CW00550065

Steel Bulwark: The Last Years of the German Panzerwaffe on the Eastern Front 1943-45 is a unique visual book providing the reader with a wide selection of rare and mostly unpublished photographs accompanied by in-depth captions. The images reveal the unfolding story of the last desperate years of the German Panzer forces – the *Panzerwaffe* – which had played a vital role in the military victories of the Nazis between 1939 and 1942. In the remaining years of the war it provided the backbone of Germany's defence. Although its strength was badly depleted following serious losses at Kursk in the summer weeks of July 1943, the *Panzerwaffe* remained committed on the battlefield in spite of the titanic struggles which took place. Throughout the last years of the war it demonstrated the German tank soldiers' superior tactical abilities and showed how they carefully utilized all available reserves and resources into building numerous variants that went into production and saw action on the battlefield. The photos portray how these formidable machines were adapted and up-gunned to face the ever-increasing enemy threat. Even when it was forced to withdraw towards the frontiers of the Reich under the constant hammer blows of enemy ground and air bombardments, it reveals how the *Panzerwaffe* played a decisive role in trying to stem the rout along the disintegrating front lines. The book is a captivating glimpse of a remarkable band of soldiers showing the evolution of their tactics and unmatched fighting vehicles. It reveals its successes and many of its defeats. Even during the last months of the war as the German Panzers withdrew ever further into their Homeland, it shows how units of the *Panzerwaffe* fought on to the grim death, hoping to hold back the superior weight of their enemy in order to win time and save their forces from ultimate destruction. The majority of the images are drawn from private collections and archives in Germany and Eastern Europe, and are previously unpublished.

About the author

Ian Baxter is a military historian who specialises in German twentieth century military history. He has written more than thirty books including *Into the Abyss: The Last Years of the Waffen-SS, From Retreat to Defeat, The Last Years of the German Army on the Eastern Front, Road to Destruction, Operation Blue and the Battle of Stalingrad 1942-43, Operation Bagration: the Destruction of Army Group Centre June-July 1944, Battle in the Baltics 1944-45: The fighting for Latvia, Lithuania and Estonia* (these last five all published by Helion), *Poland – The Eighteen Day Victory March, Panzers In North Africa, The Red Army At Stalingrad* and *German Guns of the Third Reich,* as well as contributing over 100 articles to a range of well-known military periodicals. He currently lives in Essex with Michelle and son Felix.

STEEL BULWARK

THE LAST YEARS OF THE GERMAN PANZERWAFFE ON THE EASTERN FRONT 1943–45

A Photographic History

Ian Baxter

Helion & Company Ltd

Helion & Company Limited
26 Willow Road
Solihull
West Midlands B91 1UE
England
Tel. 0121 705 3393
Fax 0121 711 4075
Email: info@helion.co.uk
Website: www.helion.co.uk

Published by Helion & Company 2009

Designed and typeset by Farr out Publications, Wokingham, Berkshire
Cover designed by Farr out Publications, Wokingham, Berkshire
Printed by The Cromwell Press Group, Trowbridge, Wiltshire

Text © Ian Baxter 2009
Photographs © HITM unless noted otherwise

ISBN 978 1 906033 40 8

British Library Cataloguing-in-Publication Data.
A catalogue record for this book is available from the British Library.

All rights reserved. No part of this publication may be reproduced, stored in a retrieval system, or transmitted, in any
form, or by any means, electronic, mechanical, photocopying, recording or otherwise, without the express written
consent of Helion & Company Limited.

For details of other military history titles published by Helion & Company Limited contact the above address, or
visit our website: http://www.helion.co.uk.

We always welcome receiving book proposals from prospective authors.

Contents

Appendices

Photographic Acknowledgements

It is with the greatest pleasure that I use this opportunity on concluding this book to thank those who helped make this volume possible. My expression of gratitude first goes to my German photographic collector, Rolf Halfen. He has been an unfailing source, supplying me with a number of photographs that were obtained from numerous private sources. Throughout the research stage of this book Rolf searched and contacted numerous collectors all over Germany, seeking a multitude of interesting and rare photographs.

Further afield in Poland I am also extremely grateful to Marcin Kaludow, my Polish photographic specialist, who supplied me with a great variety photographs that he sought from private photographic collections in Poland, Russia and the Ukraine.

Introduction

Lost victories – a brief history of the *Panzerwaffe* 1941–1942

For the invasion of Russia, code-named Barbarossa, the German Army assembled some three million men, divided into a total of 105 infantry divisions and 32 Panzer divisions. There were 3,332 tanks, over 7,000 artillery pieces, 60,000 motor vehicles and 625,000 horses. This force was distributed into three German army groups: Army Group North, commanded by Field Marshal Wilhelm Ritter von Leeb, had assembled his forces in East Prussia on the Lithuanian frontier. His *Panzergruppe*, which provided the main spearhead for the advance on Leningrad, consisted of 812 tanks. These were divided among the 1, 6 and 8. Panzer-Divisions, 3, 36. Motorised-Infantry-Divisions and the SS Motorised-Division *Totenkopf*, which formed the *Panzergruppe* reserve.

The *Panzerwaffe's* main force consisted of 410 Pz.Kpfw.I, 746 Pz.Kpfw.II, 149 Pz.Kpfw. 35(t), 623 Pz.Kpfw. 38(t), 965 Pz.Kpfw. III, and 439 Pz.Kpfw.IV. This armoured force had to rely on obsolete light tanks to provide the armoured punch.

For the Russian offensive the Panzer divisions had been slightly modified in armoured firepower. They had been in fact diluted in strength in order to form the deployment of more divisions. The planners thought that by concentrating a number of Panzer divisions together they were able to achieve a massive local superiority.

These new Panzer divisions contained one tank regiment of two, sometimes three *Abteilungen* totaling some 150-200 tanks; two motorized rifle (*schützen*) regiments, each of two battalions, whose infantry were carried in armoured halftracks or similar vehicles, and a reconnaissance battalion of three companies (one motorcycle, two armoured car). The motorized infantry divisions accompanying the Panzer divisions in the *Panzergruppe* were similarly organized, but lacked armoured support. The divisional artillery comprised of two field, one medium and one anti-tank regiment and an anti-aircraft battalion. These were all motorised and more than capable of keeping up with the fast-moving pace of the Panzers.

During the early morning of 22 June 1941 the German Army finally unleashed the maelstrom that was Barbarossa. After a month of victorious progress, the German armies were fighting on a front 1,000 miles wide. The Panzer divisions had exploited the terrain and dealt such a series of hammer blows to the Red Army that it was only a matter of time before the campaign would be over. Yet in spite of these successes the Panzer divisions were thinly spread out. Although the armoured spearheads were still achieving rapid victories on all fronts, supporting units were not keeping pace with them. Consequently, it became increasingly difficult to keep the Panzers supplied with fuel. And without fuel the drive would ground to a halt. Nevertheless, between June and late September 1941, the Panzer and motorized divisions were more or less unhindered by lack of supply, difficult terrain or bad weather conditions. However, on 6 October the first snowfall of the approaching winter was reported. It melted quickly, but turned the dirt roads into quagmires and rivers into raging torrents. The Russian autumn with its heavy rain, sleet and snow had arrived. The Panzer divisions began to slow. Wheeled vehicles soon became stuck in a sea of mud and could only advance with the aid of tracked vehicles towing them. No preparations had been made for the winter and the Panzer divisions lacked the most basic supplies for cold weather. There were no chains available for towing vehicles, and no anti-freeze for the engines coolant systems. Tank crews and infantrymen alike had no winter clothing either.

In blizzards and temperatures which fell to 30 degrees below zero, the exhausted Panzer divisions soon ran out of fuel and ammunition, and were compelled to break off their attack within sight of Moscow. On 6 December all plans to capture the Russian capital in 1941 had to be abandoned.

By 22 December only 405 tanks were operational in front of Moscow with 780 out of action, but repairable. By the end of the year, the Germans reported the loss of 2,735 tanks plus 847 replacements since 22 June. Not even 1,400 operational and damaged tanks remained of the once-powerful and proud Panzer divisions.

By the end of 1941 the battle weary divisions of the *Panzerwaffe*, which had taken part in Operation Barbarossa, were no longer fit to fight. Mobile operations had consequently ground to a halt. Fortunately for the exhausted Panzer crews and supporting units no mobile operations had been planed during the winter of 1941, let alone for 1942. In the freezing arctic temperatures the majority of the Panzer divisions were pulled out of their stagnant defensive positions and transferred to France, to rest, reorganize and retrain.

In spite of the terrible problems that faced the badly depleted Panzer divisions, back in Germany production of tanks still increased. In order to overcome the mammoth task of defeating the Red Army more Panzer divisions were being raised, and motorized divisions converted into Panzergrenadier divisions. Although equipping the *Panzerwaffe* was a slow expensive process, it was undertaken effectively with the introduction of a number of new fresh divisions being deployed on the front lines.

However, by the beginning of the summer offensive in May 1942, not all the Panzer divisions were fully equipped and ready for combat. Some of the older units for instance did not even have their losses from the winter offensive of 1941 replaced and were not ready for any type of full-scale operation. Worn out and depleted Panzer divisions were therefore relegated to Army Group North or Army Group Centre where they were hastily deployed for a series of defensive actions instead. The best-equipped Panzer divisions were shifted south to Army Group South for operations through the Caucasus. This was entrusted to the two Panzer Armies – 1st and 4th – that were to spearhead the drive. By May 1942 most of the Panzer divisions involved were up to nearly eighty five percent of their original fighting strength, and been equipped with Pz.Kpfw.III's and Pz.Kpfw.IV's.

With renewed confidence the summer offensive, codenamed 'Operation Blau', opened up in southern Russia. Some 15 Panzer divisions and Panzergrenadier divisions of the 1st and 4th Armies, together with Italian, Rumanian and Hungarian formations moved into action. In just two days the leading spearheads had pushed 150km deep into the enemy lines and began to cut off the city of Voronezh. The city fell on 7 July. The two Panzer armies then converged with all their might on Stalingrad. It seemed that the Russians were now doomed. With an air of confidence Hitler decided to abandon the armoured advance on Stalingrad and embark on an encirclement operation down on the Don. The 6th Army was to continue to capture Stalingrad without any real Panzer support and would fight a bloody battle of attrition there. Eventually the fighting became so fierce it embroiled some 21 German divisions including six Panzer and Panzergrenadier divisions.

The 6th Army soon became encircled and three hurriedly reorganized understrength Panzer divisions were thrown into a relief operation. By 19 December the 6th Panzer Division had fought its way to within 50km of Stalingrad. But under increasing Russian pressure the relief operation failed. The 6th Panzer Division and remnants of the 4th Panzer Army were forced to retreat, leaving the 6th Army in the encircled city to its fate. Some 94,000 soldiers surrendered on 2 February 1943. With them the 14th, 16th, and 24th Panzer Divisions, and the 3rd, 29th, and 60th Panzergrenadier Divisions were decimated.

The end now seemed destined to unfold, but still more resources were poured into the Panzer divisions. Throughout the early cold months of 1943, the *Panzerwaffe* built up strength, and the badly-depleted Panzer divisions refitted. By the summer the Germans fielded some 24 Panzer divisions on the Eastern Front alone. This was a staggering transformation of a Panzer force that had lost immeasurable amounts of armour in less than two years of combat. Hitler now intended to risk his precious Panzerwaffe in what became the largest tank battle of World War Two, Operation *Zitadelle*.

During the *Panzerwaffe's* victorious drive through southern Russia a line of PzKpfw III's, with an Ausf J in the foreground, can be seen using a gradient in a field as concealment across the vast expanse of the Russian steppe.

A PzKpfw III has halted in a field and two crewmembers watch as a number of Russian soldiers surrender. By 3 July 1941 the battle of the frontier in Russia was over and armoured and infantry units were pushing forward at breakneck speed achieving their tactical bounds. As a result thousands of Soviet prisoners were captured.

A PzKpfw III Ausf L advances through a field leaving a trail of devastation in its wake. This vehicle belongs to the 26th Panzer Division. During the opening stages of the invasion of the Soviet Union in June 1941, there were some 956 PzKpfw III's.

Various vehicles including halftracks, tanks and motorcycles are purposely spaced out across the Russian steppe in order to minimise the threat of aerial attack.

A PzKpfw II Ausf F and a PzKpfw III Ausf J have halted on a road in southern Russia. Two PzKpfw III crewmembers watch a number of motorcycle combinations crossing a field. Due to the high numbers of motorcyclists killed in battle, gradually during the war motorcyclists were relegated to communication and reconnaissance duties.

A halftrack towing what appears to be a PaK 40 across a field during operations in southern Russia in 1942. This anti-tank gun proved it worth in Russia and was more than capable of disabling heavy Soviet armour.

Two photographs showing a typical scene during the summer of 1941 showing a congested road full of vehicles and horse drawn transport. Note a column of PzKpfw 38 (t)`s halted on the road. For the opening attack on Russia the *Panzerwaffe* employed some 623 of these Czech built tanks.

The crew of a PzKpfw 38 (t) pose for the camera. It was soon realised during the invasion of Russia that the PzKpfw 38 (t) was no match against the growing superior enemy armour, and by 1942 these light tanks were finally relegated to second line duties.

A PzKpfw III moves across a dusty field during operations in the early summer of 1942. During the first months of the invasion of Russia the PzKpfw III showed its worth. However, against formidable Russian armour such as the T-34 medium and the KV-1 heavy tanks, the PzKpfw III was soon recognized as an inadequate weapon in the ranks of the *Panzerwaffe*.

A photograph probably taken in southern Russia on the Don prior to the battle of Stalingrad showing two PzKpfw III tanks halted near two dwellings in the summer of 1942.

PART I

Fighting withdrawal

Bitter fighting in the South

In June 1943, 21 Panzer divisions, including four *Waffen-SS* divisions and two Panzergrenadier divisions were being prepared for Operation *Zitadelle* in the Kursk salient. For this massive attack the *Panzerwaffe* was able to muster in early July 17 divisions and two brigades with no less than 1,715 Panzers and 147 Sturmegeschutz III (StuG) assault guns. Each division averaged some 98 Panzers and self-propelled anti-tank guns. The new Pz.Kpfw.V '*Panther*' Ausf.A made its debut, despite its production problems.

Putting together such a strong force was a great achievement, but the *Panzerwaffe* of 1943 was unlike those armoured forces that had victoriously steamrolled across western Russia two years earlier. The losses during the previous winter had resulted in the drastic reductions in troop strength. Despite the *Panzerwaffe's* impressive array of firepower, this shortage of infantry was to lead to Panzer units being required to take on more ambitious tasks normally preserved for the infantry. In fact, to make matters worse, by the time the final date had been set for the attack as the 4 July, the Red Army knew the German plans and they had made their preparations. For three long months there had been extensive building and various other preparations to counter the German attack. Improved intelligence allowed Russian commanders to predict exactly the strategic focal point of the German attack. The *Panzerwaffe*, however, was determined to rejuvenate their Blitzkrieg tactics, but the immense preparations that had gone into constructing the Soviet defences meant that the *Panzerwaffe* would never succeed in penetrating into the strategic depths of the Red Army fortifications with any overriding success.

When the attack was finally unleashed in the pre-dawn light of 5 July 1943, the Germans were stunned by the dogged defence of their Red foe. The battle was unlike any other engagement they had previously encountered. A German grenadier wrote: "The Red Army soldiers refused to give up. Nor did they panic in the face of our roaring Tiger tanks. The Soviets were cunning in every way. They allowed our tanks to rumble past their well-camouflaged foxholes and then sprang out to deal with the German grenadiers following in its wake. Constantly our tanks and assault guns had to turn back to relieve the stranded and often exhausted grenadiers".

The initial phases of the Soviet defensive action at Kursk were often crude, messy and costly, but in a tactical and operational sense achieved their objectives. Within only a matter of days, they had ground down the mighty *Panzerwaffe* and threw its offensive timetable off schedule. Through sheer weight of Soviet strength and stubborn combat along an ever-extending front, the German mobile units were finally forced to a standstill.

The losses that the *Panzerwaffe* sustained at Kursk were so immense that it undoubtedly led to the German Army taking their first steps of its slow retreat back towards Germany. The Russians had managed to destroy no less than 30 divisions, seven of which were Panzer. German reinforcements were insufficient to replace the staggering losses, so they fought on under-strength.

The reverberations caused by the defeat at Kursk meant that German forces in the south bore the brunt of the heaviest Soviet drive. Both the Russian Voronezh and Steppe Fronts possessed massive local superiority against everything the Germans had on the battlefield, and this included their diminishing resources of tanks and assault guns. The *Panzerwaffe* were now duty-bound to improvise with what they had at their disposal and try to maintain themselves in the field, and in doing so they hoped to wear the enemy's offensive capacity. But in the south where the weight of the Soviet effort was directed, Army Group South's line began breaking and threatened to be ripped wide open. Stiff defensive action was now the stratagem placed upon the *Panzerwaffe*, but they lacked sufficient reinforcements and the strength of their armoured units dwindled steadily as they tried to hold back the Russian might.

During the first uneasy weeks of August 1943 the 1st Panzer Army and *Armeeabteilung* Kempf fought to hold ground along the Donets River whilst the final battle of Kharkov was fought out. Further north near the battered town of Akhtyrka the 4th Panzer Army was also fighting a frenzied battle of attrition. Along the whole Russian front massive Soviet artillery bombardments would sweep the German lines and inflict considerable casualties on both infantry and armoured vehicles. Throughout August and September the *Panzerwaffe* tried frantically to hold on to the receding front line. With just over 1000 Panzers operating in southern Russia the Germans were seriously understrength and still further depleted by vehicles being constantly taken out for repair. Along many areas of the front, high losses resulted from inadequate supplies and not the skill of the defenders.

In other areas of the Russian front the situation was just the same. Both Army Group Centre and Army Group North were trying desperately to hold the Soviets back from breaking through their lines. Replacements continued to trickle through to help bolster the under strength *Panzerwaffe*. But in truth, the average new Panzer soldier that was freshly recruited was not as well trained as his predecessors during the early part of the campaign in Russia. Nevertheless, as with many Panzer men they were characterized by high morale and a determination to do their duty.

In almost three months since the defeat at Kursk Army Centre and South had been pushed back an average distance of 150 miles on a 650 mile front. Despite heavy resistance in many sectors of the front the Soviets lost no time in exploiting the fruits of regaining as much territory as possible. In Army Group South where the frontlines threatened to completely cave in under intense enemy pressure, frantic appeals to Hitler were made by Field Marshal Manstein to withdraw his forces across the Dnieper River. What followed was a fighting withdrawal that degenerated into a race with the Russians for possession of the river. Whilst the Panzer divisions covered the rear, the army group's columns withdrew on selected river crossing points at Cherkassy, Dniepropetrovsk, Kiev, Kanev and Krmenchug, leaving behind a burnt a blasted wasteland during their retreat.

The crossing of the Dnieper River before the battered and worn front disintegrated into total ruin was one of the major achievements of Field Marshal von Manstein's career. The Germans still believed they could stabilize the front, but the Soviet numerical superiority was far too great. By trying to hold the east side of the Dnieper the Germans had sapped most of the strength out of Army Group South and Centre. The *Panzerwaffe* was now required to try and perform yet another reversal of Germany's misfortunes in the East. In most areas of the front Panzers crews were no longer to adopt any risky offensive tactics but to use a delaying and blocking strategy instead. As the third winter fast approached they hoped that the arctic conditions too would impede the onset of another Russian offensive.

Winter and summer battles 1943-44

The winter of 1943 opened up with an exasperating series of deliberations for the *Panzerwaffe*. Much of its concerns were preventing the awesome might of the Red Army with what little they had available at their disposal. Yet, in October and November of 1943 only five Panzer divisions and one SS Panzer division were sent as replacements on the Eastern Front. Of these, only the 1st SS Panzer Division LSSAH and 1st Panzer Division were full strength with two battalions totalling some 180 tanks. The 14th, 24th and 25th Panzer Divisions had about 100 tanks and assault guns in one single battalion. During the winter of 1943 all units on the Eastern Front averaged 2,000 tanks, of which only 800 of them were regarded as combat ready at any one time. It was indeed a very small force for such a large front to cover, but despite the depressing statistics the German tank soldier was still infused with confidence and the ability to hold ground. However, by early November the Russians once more began to roll across the wet and snowy plains in the south. In the wake of a massive artillery bombardment, Soviet forces hit the centre of the German front with such a force it ripped it open. In just two days the 4th Panzer Army front around Lutezh collapsed. During the night of 5 November the battle swept through Kiev, and the next morning Panzers supported by infantry retreated. Lacking reserves of any kind armoured vehicles of the 4th Panzer Army were helpless as they tried to defend the rear of its forces. For the next two weeks a bitter and bloody battle raged.

On 20 November the First Panzer Army, which had been fighting continuously for days in the region around Nikopol, reported to the Army Group that their strength had sunk to the lowest tolerable level. Glum as the situation was, armoured units were compelled to try and fill the gaps left by the infantry, and hold the front to the grim death. Throughout December the *Panzerwaffe* fought well, and at times even succeeded surprising Red Army forces with a number of daring attacks of their own. Although handicapped from the onset by their lack of reserves the 4th Panzer Army managed to spearhead and capture or destroy 700 tanks and 668 guns in early January 1944.

Throughout January and February the winter did nothing to impede the Soviet offensives from grinding further west. At the beginning of March 1944, Army Group A and South still held about half the ground between the Dnieper and Bug, but in a number of areas the front was buckling under the constant strain of repeated Soviet attacks. As a consequence Army Group South was being slowly pressed westwards, its Panzers still unable to strike a decisive counter-blow because of the Führer order to stand fast on unsuitable positions. By 24 March the Russians had spearheaded a drive to the Dniester, and a few days later were penetrating the foothills of the Carpathians. *Panzerwaffe* units that were refused permission by Hitler to withdraw found themselves tied down trying in vain to hold back the Soviet avalanche. These battles became known to the Panzer soldiers as the 'cauldron battles' or *Kesselschlachten*.

By April mud finally brought an end to almost continuous fighting in the south, and there was respite for the *Panzerwaffe* in some areas of the front. Once more, despite the setbacks, there was a genuine feeling of motivation within the ranks of the *Panzerwaffe*. There was renewed determination to keep the 'Red menace' out of the Homeland. In addition, confidence was further bolstered by the efforts of the armaments industry as they begun producing many new vehicles for the Eastern Front. In fact during 1944 the *Panzerwaffe* were better supplied with equipment during any other time on the Eastern Front, thanks to the armaments industry. In total some 20,000 fighting vehicles including 8,328 medium and heavy tanks, 5,751 assault guns, 3,617 tank destroyers and 1, 246 self-propelled artillery carriages of various types reached the Eastern Front. Included in these new arrivals were the second generation of tank-destroyers, the Jagdpanzer IV, followed by the Hetzer and then the Jagpanther and Jagdtiger. In fact, tank-destroyers and assault guns would soon outnumber the tanks, which was confirmation of the *Panzerwaffe*'s obligation to performing a defensive role against overwhelming opposition. All of these vehicles would have to be irrevocably stretched along a very thin Eastern Front, with many of them rarely reaching the proper operating level. Panzer divisions too were often broken up and split among hastily constructed battle groups or *Kampfgruppe* drawn from a motley collection of armoured formations. But still these battle groups were put into the line operating well below strength. The demands that were put upon the *Panzerwaffe* during the spring and summer of 1944 were immeasurable. The constant employment, coupled with the nightmare of not having enough supplies, was a worry that perpetually festered in the minds of the commanders. The Red Army encouraged by the German's dire situation was now mounting bolder operations aimed directly against the German front.

With renewed confidence Soviet commanders began drawing up plans for a massive concentration of forces along the entire frontline in central Russia. The new summer offensive was to be called 'Operation Bagration' and its objective was to annihilate Army Group Centre.

On the morning of 22 June, the third anniversary of the Soviet invasion, 'Operation *Bagration*' was launched against Army Group Centre. The three German armies opposing them had thirty-seven divisions, weakly supported by armour, against 166 divisions, supported by 2,700 tanks and 1,300 assault guns. At the end of the first week of *Bagration* the three German armies had lost between them nearly 200,000 men and 900 tanks; 9th Army and the 3rd Panzer Army were almost decimated. The remnants of the shattered armies trudged back west in order to try and rest and refit what was left of its Panzer units and build new defensive lines. Any plans to regain the initiative on the Eastern Front were doomed forever.

Two photographs taken in sequence showing a Waffen-SS SdKfz 251 halftrack moving through a wheat field transporting SS grenadiers into battle during the summer of 1943. [Michael Cremin]

Armoured vehicles consisting of two stationary SdKfz 251 halftracks and a PzKpfw V Panther halted in a wheat field. The Panther first appeared at Kursk in July 1943, making a rather inauspicious operational debut. By 1944, however, following a number of successful improvements, it dominated the battlefield. [Michael Cremin]

A Sturmgeschütz III or StuG III Ausf F assault gun has been loaded onto a train for transportation to the Eastern Front. This vehicle is equipped with the longer barrelled 7.5cm StuK 40 L/48 cannon, which both necessitated modification of the frontal superstructure and increased the vehicle's overall weight to 21.3 tons.

A StuG III has been concealed in some undergrowth during summer operations in 1943. Despite the longer 7.5cm barrel this assault gun was continually hard-pressed on the battlefield and constantly called upon for offensive and defensive fire support, where it was gradually compelled to operate increasingly in an anti-tank role.

A new PzKpfw IV has just arrived on the Eastern Front. The PzKpfw IV became the most popular Panzer in the *Panzerwaffe* and remained in production throughout the war. Originally the PzKpfw IV was designed as an infantry support tank, but soon proved to be so diverse and effective that it earned a unique offensive and defensive role on the battlefield.

Two photographs showing Panthers on a training ground being put through their paces. Despite the tank being plagued by mechanical problems the *Panzerwaffe* deployed two Panther-equipped tank battalions for the Kursk offensive and these fought on the southern front.

A group of Waffen-SS troops pose for the camera with their SdKfz 251 halftrack whilst operating in Russia in 1943. All the men appear to be wearing their winter reversibles.

The crew of an unidentified Tiger tank battalion have halted somewhere in Russia. The PzKpfw VI Tiger tank was probably the most famous Panzer in the *Panzerwaffe* and was nicknamed by the troops the 'furniture van' because of its size.

Three Panthers on a training exercise. The leading Panther has the factory number '116' painted in white on the side of the turret.

The crew of an SdKfz 250/1 passes through a field and are all captured on film facing the camera. The SdKfz 250 was designed purely to provide armoured reconnaissance troops in the Panzer and Panzergrenadier divisions with better off-road performance than the SdKfz 222. These light armoured personnel carriers normally carried six troops and were armed with either an MG34 or MG42 machine gun, which can be seen in this photograph with splinter shield

Two crewman stand beside their Panther during a training exercise. This variant mounts six smoke candle dischargers, three on each side of the turret. These were discontinued in production during June 1943. However, some Panthers still carried them for a number of months until they were finally removed.

General Heinz Guderian and staff inspect a Tiger tank in 1943. One of the Panzer men opens the commander's cupola hatch and shows the General the internal view of the commander's compartment.

Two PzKpfw IVs lead an armoured column through a field during summer operations in 1943. For the majority of the war the PzKpfw IV was certainly a match for its opponent's heavy tanks and quickly and effectively demonstrated its capability on the battlefield.

An interesting image showing one of the independent Tiger battalions undertaking mechanical work on a Tiger from SS schwere Panzer Abteilung 101 in 1943. The large portal crane is being used to remove the heavy turret for repairs.

An impressive photograph showing a StuG III leading an armoured column. Because the StuG III was constantly in great demand in Russia Hitler ordered that the assault gun be up-gunned and up-armoured with a longer more potent 7.5cm gun. This more powerful assault gun went into production in mid-1942. The Ausf F variant mounted a 7.5cm StuK 40 L/43 gun. The following year the final StuG variant, the Ausf G, entered service with the *Panzerwaffe*.

Here a Nashorn 8.8cm heavy Panzerjäger is photographed at a maintenance workshop, probably in Germany in 1944. Between early 1943 and March 1945, only 474 Nashorns were produced.

PzKpfw IVs advance through a field during the Battle of Kursk in July 1943. The *Panzerwaffe*'s failure at Kursk resulted in huge losses of tanks and material. After the battle only five Wehrmacht Panzer divisions and one Waffen-SS Panzer division were sent as replacements to the Eastern Front in late 1943. Note the protective side-skirts or Schürzen on the vehicles.

A Tiger tank is embroiled in heavy fighting during the Battle of Kursk. The battle was the largest tank, air, infantry and artillery battle in history and it was a turning point in the war for the Germans.

Troops belonging to the 4. SS Panzer division rest in an area that has been razed to the ground by heavy fighting. An SdKfz 8 halftrack and a PzKpfw III from the 4th Company of a Panzer regiment have halted near a trench whilst SS troops pause and have a cigarette.

A PzKpfw IV moves hastily along a dusty road somewhere in southern Russia in the summer of 1943. Note the rack fitted with jerry cans on the turret roof, indicating the vehicle is in for a long road march.

A halftrack makes its way over a pontoon bridge during the withdrawal from the area around Kursk. By August 1943, with the *Panzerwaffe* desperately trying to hold onto their lines, a massive gap was wrenched open by the Soviets west of Kursk, enabling thousands of troops to pour through.

A PzKpfw IV can be seen leading an armoured column during operations in Russia during the summer of 1943. After Kursk the PzKpfw IV played a prominent role in the desperate attempt to halt the Soviet onslaught. Even though these powerful tanks were vastly outnumbered they performed creditably with the Panzer divisions in which they served.

A halftrack armed with a mounted 2cm Flak gun moves along a dusty road. Anti-aircraft defences came into prominence from late 1941, as the Soviet Air Force started to inflict heavy casualties. By 1943 and early 1944, both the Wehrmacht and Waffen-SS mechanised formations had become well equipped with flak guns.

An SS soldier scours the terrain ahead in his stationary SdKfz 251/9 halftrack. This vehicle is armed with the short 7.5cm KwK 37 L/24, which was mounted on the PzKpfw IV before it was up-armoured with the 7.5cm L/43 and L/48. Note the kill rings on the barrel. [Michael Cremin]

A Tiger I in some undergrowth during a lull in fighting on the Eastern Front, probably in 1943. The Tiger entered service in August 1942 and soon gained a superb fighting record. The mighty Tigers played a key role in the German offensive at Kursk.

Soldiers belonging to the SS 2nd Panzer Division 'Das Reich' division during operations in Russia in the summer of 1943. Following the Battle of Kursk in July 1943, part of the Division was re-titled Kampfgruppe Das Reich, and officially known as Kampfgruppe Lammerding. The rest of the Division was transferred to the West for a refit. [Michael Cremin]

A column of PzKpfw IV's move along a typical road in southern Russia during operations in the early winter of 1943. Stowed on the rear of the engine deck of the leading vehicle are fuel drums. The vast distances in which these vehicles were compelled to travel meant that quite often tracked vehicles outstripped fuel supplies, prompting crews to carry reserves.

A PzKpfw II Ausf L 'Lynx' company commander's vehicle during the winter of 1943. These were very rare PzKpfw II vehicles and only 100 of them were ever produced. They were assigned to the 4th Panzer Division, although the 9th Panzer Division was the only other unit to receive a full company.

A StuG III Ausf G in a field with a full covering of winter whitewash paint. By 1943 the StuG III had become an extremely common assault gun in the *Panzerwaffe* on the Eastern Front. Its low profile and mechanical reliability saw its employment grow on the battlefield.

Vehicles are being loaded onto flatbed railway cars destined for the frontline. Moving vehicles by rail became a common requirement by the *Panzerwaffe* in late 1943. It enabled the Panzer divisions to move from one front to another quickly and effectively without wear and tear.

An 8.8cm flak gun is being towed by an artillery tractor through the snow. The *Panzerwaffe* relied heavily on the various light and heavy armoured vehicles for transportation. Maintaining the momentum of an advance was vital to its success and, without transport, the whole advance might stall.

A Panther crew poses for the camera with their vehicle in late 1943. Despite the unfavorable events that transpired on the Eastern Front during the last two years of the war the Panther combined a formidable mix of firepower, armour and mobility, outclassing most of its opponents, including the Russian T-34/76.

An SS crew wearing winter reversibles grey side out can be seen in the fighting compartment of a stationary Hummel. The Hummel mounted a standard 15cm heavy field howitzer in a lightly armoured fighting compartment built on the chassis of a PzKpfw III/IV. This heavy self-propelled gun carried eighteen 15cm rounds, but was a potent weapon against Soviet armour.

Tiger tanks are being replenished with ammunition. Shells are being carefully unloaded and passed through the hatch. In spite the German military reversal on the Eastern Front the *Panzerwaffe* would extensively use the Tiger in a number of prominent roles in both major offensive and defensive employments.

Two photographs showing Tiger tanks with an application of winter whitewash paint over a coating of Zimmerit anti-magnetic mine paste. By early 1944 the Tiger continued to play an important, mainly defensive, role.

Two photographs showing Panzerjäger Tiger or Ferdinand Elefant tank destroyers that have been chocked and secured ready for their journey by rail. Due to their sheer size and weight, no more than six of these vehicles were permitted to be loaded on one train. These were interspersed with two flatcars to avoid overloading of the train, and also to prevent overloading of the bridges.

Here a well camouflaged Ferdinand Elefant has run out of fuel. This tank destroyer was capable of defeating all types of Soviet tanks, but the vehicle lacked cross-country mobility and was prone to breakdowns. Also, with no secondary armament they were vulnerable to infantry armed with magnetic mines and charges.

Members of the crew of a Sturmpanzer Brummbär sit proudly atop their vehicle. This was a powerful infantry support weapon developed in consequence of experiences fighting in Stalingrad. Armed with a powerful 15cm StuH 43 L/12 gun, 306 examples were built.

A 15cm schweres Infanteriegeschütz 33, which mounted the 15cm sIG33 infantry gun on a PzKpfw 38(t) chassis.
90 of these vehicles were built, serving with the sIG companies within Panzergrenadier regiments.

A Ferdinand Elefant has halted inside a village. The *Panzerwaffe* placed great value on the new second generation of tank destroyers, and much was expected of them during the last year of the war. In April 1944 Schwere Panzerjäger Abteilung 653 sent its Elefant tank destroyers by rail where they were deployed with the 1st Panzer Army, part of Army Group North Ukraine, near Ternopol.

A transport train loaded with a Tiger I heading for another part of the front in Russia.

A Tiger Ausf E attached to the 3rd Company, schwere Panzer Abteilung 502 fords a river during summer operations in 1943. Such heavy tanks did not fare well on such terrain, but it was often the quickest method of reaching areas often impassable with other armoured vehicles.

Two crewmembers pose for the camera in front of a well-camouflaged Jagdpanzer 38 (t) Hezter Tank destroyer. This vehicle became the most advanced tank destroyer in the *Panzerwaffe's* arsenal. With its distinctive silhouetted armoured superstructure it carried a deadly 7.5cm PaK 39 L/48 gun on a specially widened PzKpfw 38 (t) chassis. By the summer of 1944, it began joining the anti-tank battalions.

A Hummel self-propelled gun being prepared for transportation. This popular vehicle was a very effective weapon in the *Panzerwaffe*. A total of 666 Hummel's were built until the programme was finally terminated in 1944.

A Tiger tank being put through its paces in front of an audience in the summer of 1943. This vehicle, with the tactical number 300 painted on the side of the turret, was attached to the 3rd Company, schwere Panzer Abteilung 503. The schwere Panzer Abteilung 503 saw action at Kursk, and in late 1943 was made part of Panzer Regiment 'Bäke', a special battle group which fought in several brutal actions in the Dnieper sector near Cherkassy. It remained attached to 'Bäke' until April 1944, when it was finally withdrawn to the West for a refit.

A Panther halted on a road. One of the crew poses for the camera sprawled out across the vehicle's cleaning tube. The Panther still retains its old smoke candle dischargers that were fitted on either side of the turret. This practice ceased in June 1943 after a reported incident earlier that year, when enemy small arms had set off the dischargers, incapacitating the crew.

Two photographs showing Panthers being transported by rail to the front line. Transporting armour by rail was undertaken frequently in Russia by the *Panzerwaffe*. Not only did it save time on the huge distances that had to be covered, but it also allowed Panzer divisions to move from one part of the front to another quickly and effectively. In fact, a principal factor in the success of the Panzer divisions speed and mobility was attributed to rail transport.

Two Waffen-SS soldiers smile for the camera inside a Volkswagen armoured car during operations in the summer of 1944. In the distance is a stationary Panther and an SdKfz 251 halftrack. [Michael Cremin]

A column of Panthers roll along a road, destined for the front lines. By 1944 the disparity of armoured vehicles meant that Panzers like the Panther had to wage continuous defensive battles in order to wear down the enemy in a war of attrition. [Michael Cremin]

A Panther Ausf G moves along a typical Russian road after a heavy down pour. The Panther passes an exhausted horse that has become stuck in the mire. Despite the *Panzerwaffe*'s attempts to make their armoured force fully mechanised, a great number of horses were still used in 1944 to carry soldiers and equipment to the front. As a result many of them perished through physical exertion, hunger, or were killed in battle. [Michael Cremin]

An SS soldier can be seen standing in his SdKfz 222 armoured reconnaissance car during operations in the summer of 1944. [Michael Cremin]

A crewman poses for the camera next to his StuG III Ausf F. Track links can be seen attached to the vehicle for additional armoured protection. Note the protective covering placed on the end of the 7.5cm gun's muzzle break to prevent dust particles and other foreign matter contaminating the gun tube.

The crew of a StuG III pose for the camera in some woodland. From 1943 until the end of the war the assault guns were increasingly absorbed into the Panzer units, Panzer and Panzer grenadier divisions of the Wehrmacht and Waffen-SS.

A 10.5cm Sturmhaubitz 42 displaying a very full coating of Zimmerit anti-magnetic mine paste. For additional armoured protection track links have been bolted to the vehicles glacis. The StuH 42 was used within StuG brigades to provide additional firepower both in attack and defence.

Two crewmembers can be seen sitting with their Wespe howitzer on board a flat bed railway car. Note the specially constructed rack to carry jerry cans of fuel for long road marches. This popular vehicle was armed with a 10.5cm leFH 18/2 L/28 gun and protected by a lightly armoured superstructure mounted on a chassis of a PzKpfw II. This vehicle served in armoured artillery battalions but was lightly armoured, and as a result many of them were lost in battle.

Three photographs of Tiger I's, all of which are seen here during the summer of 1943. Between August 1942 and September 1944, some 1354 Tiger I's were constructed. During this period, these vehicles constantly demonstrated both the lethality of their 8.8cm guns and their invulnerability against Soviet anti-tank shells.

During the winter of 1943 a Tiger tank can be seen halted out in the Russian steppe with the crew preparing to change tracks for cross-country combat operations. A Fiesler Storch reconnaissance aircraft has landed nearby.

PART II

Panzerwaffe in Retreat

Defensive battles in the East

In spite of the success of Operation Bagration and the complete collapse of Army Group Centre the Red Army still did not equal the *Panzerwaffe* in either performance or tactical ability on the battlefield. Though Soviet armaments production saw some 29,000 tanks and assault guns being produced for the frontlines alone in 1944, the *Panzerwaffe* still possessed a slight advantage in their vehicles, notably tanks like the new Tiger E and the King Tiger B. These were undoubtedly formidable fighting machines whose arrival at the front was a welcome relief to the already hard-pressed *Panzerwaffe*. Nonetheless the production of the new second generation of tanks did nothing to alleviate the overall predicament that was increasingly festering along the entire battered and worn Eastern Front. With too few of them delivered, Tigers, Panthers, assault guns and tank destroyer crews found that they were too thinly stretched to make any considerable dent against the growing tank might of the Red Army. What followed during the last weeks of July was a frantic attempt by the *Panzerwaffe* to stem the rout of the Soviet drive into Poland. Army Group North Ukraine tried its best to contain its slender position on the River Bug, whilst remnants of Army Group Centre tried with all available resources to create a solid front line Kaunas, Bialystok-Brest and assemble what was left of its forces on both its flanks. But between Army Group Centre and Army Group North German positions were depleted. The mauled 3rd Panzer Army had been fighting continuously in the area and even managed to capture and secure a number of villages in the area. In late July it captured Schaulen and then advanced on Mitau. The 3rd Panzer Army ordered the 7th Panzer Division to press on further and attack the Soviet 6th Guards Tanks Army in the area south of Kovno. The operation was very risky, but the *Panzerwaffe* once again demonstrated their effectiveness on the battlefield. The 3rd Panzer Army desperately tried to hold Kovno, fearing that loosing this Russian province would ensure the collapse of the Baltic States. On 31 July the Red Army pushed forward using their newly-won freedom of manoeuvre in the direction of the East Prussian border. Meanwhile the 6th Panzer Division blocked the route towards Griskabudis, whilst Panzergrenadier Brigade von Werthen blocked the south bank of the Memel near Zapyskis. A few days later the Red Army unleashed a considerable number of tanks either side of Nova where the 6th Panzer Division was operating. What followed was the battle of Kovno.

Although German *Panzerwaffe* commanders were fully aware of the fruitless attempts by their forces to establish a defensive line, the crews followed instructions implicitly in a number of areas to halt the Soviet drive. Again and again Panzer units fought to the grim death. In Latvia Bagramyan's 1st Baltic Front had meanwhile broken through to the Gulf of Riga, totally isolating Army Group North. From the west the 3rd Panzer Army bolstered by some 400 tanks and assault guns viciously counterattacked in the direction of Shauliya and Yelgava. The counterattack spearheaded by XXXX and XXXIX Panzer Corps was code-named 'Operation Doppelkopf'. Part of the German plan was to initially cut off the Soviet troops on the Baltic coast, and re-establish a tenuous 20-mile wide corridor connecting Army Groups Centre and North. The main objective of the attack was to re-take the key road-junction of Šiauliai, but the Panzers soon ran into heavy defensive positions held grimly by the 1st Baltic Front. Despite its best efforts and the mauling of the 4th, 5th, 14th Panzer divisions, and the once vaunted Grossdeutschland Panzergrenadier Division, they only made slow progress against the very strong and resilient Russian 51st, 2nd Guards and 5th Guards Tank Armies. By 20 August the German advance had stalled with heavy losses. But determined as ever to hold back the Red Army onslaught, another attack was launched. Within a matter of hours well-sited Russian anti-tank gunners and tank crews brought the German Panzer attack to a flaming halt.

After a brief respite along the German front, the Soviets began preparing for the Baltic Strategic Offensive. On 14 September the German front lines in Latvia were brought under heavy systematic bombardment as Red Army troops were poised to attack on the Riga axis. The *Panzerwaffe* defending the area was aware of the geographical significance if the Baltic States were captured. Although the German defenders attempted to stall the massive Russian onslaught, by 15 September, the 3rd Baltic Front had ripped open and decimated much of the German lines in the east. From the south the Soviets were threatening the road to Riga, where the German X Corps had been heavily engaged in bitter fighting. Within a matter of days ten of the eighteen German divisions employed in the area around Riga to halt the Red Army had been reduced to a motley assorted collection of disjointed battle groups.

Heavily mauled German forces were now compelled to pull back west of Riga. As they prepared a new line of defence, the Soviets meanwhile were planning to launch another attack, this time southwards in preparation for a major drive towards Memel by the 1st Baltic Front. In just two weeks the 1st Baltic Front reached Memel while the 2nd and 3rd Baltic Fronts closed in on Riga. What was left of Army Group North, which amounted to some thirty-three divisions, was ordered to withdraw into the Courland peninsular and the Memel perimeter. Here valuable Panzer divisions that could have been used elsewhere on the front were needlessly ordered to hold out and become trapped so that they could tie down large parts of the 1st Baltic Front.

These were agonising moments for the German forces in the East. Despite the huge losses and lack of reserves many still remained resolute stemming the Soviet drive east, even if it meant giving ground and fighting in Poland – the last bastion of defence before the Reich.

Action in Poland

Between June and September 1944 the Germans had sustained some one million casualties. To make good their losses many of the exhausted undermanned divisions were conscripted of old men and low-grade troops. The method of recruitment generally did not produce very good results. Not only were the number of recruits simply insufficient, but the enlistment of volunteers in to the German Army was beginning to show signs of strain and exhaustion. In the *Panzerwaffe* too many of the replacement crews did not have sufficient time to be properly trained and as a result losses soared. Lack of fuel, not enough spare parts, coupled with the lack of trained crews all played a major part in reducing the effectiveness of the *Panzerwaffe* in the final year of the war.

Yet despite this deficiency in men and equipment the German Army did manage to slow down the Russian drive in the East, if only temporarily. On the central sector of the Eastern Front the remnants of the once vaunted Army Group Centre had steadily withdrawn across the Polish border westwards in July 1944. Its exhausted troops had been forced back towards Kaunas, the Neman River and Bialystok. By early August the Red Army was advancing in a wedge toward Warsaw. The XX Army Corps immediately deployed a battalion to the newly formed IV Waffen-SS Corps, due to the fact that the forces of the Waffen-SS Panzer Division 'Totenkopf' had been given the dutiful task supporting the right flank of the 2nd Army in the direction of the Vistula. The Red Army were now preparing to establish a bridgehead across the Vistula to the west and hoped that a rapid drive on the Polish capital, Warsaw, would bring a quick conclusion to the war. As Soviet forces spearheaded their troops across the Polish border toward the Vistula they used extremely rapid mobile forces. By using the heavy motorization it relieved the physical responsibility of the infantry. In many areas east of the Vistula the Russians met almost no resistance. During their almost unhindered drive they were able to cross the Warsaw – Lukow – Brest and Warsaw – Siedlce rail lines and cut off the 2nd Army from the important supply rail lines. The capture of the rail lines severely delayed units of the 4th Panzer Division from receiving reinforcements and ammunition. Consequently, much of the ammunition had to be brought by road risking the support column from being attacked by Red Army fighter bombers that were prowling the skies.

The 4th Panzer Division had been given the role of trying to stem the advance of the Soviet 2nd Tank Army. The division was divided into two battle groups. In total they had 98 combat vehicles available for action, only 69 of which belonged to the division. During its first encounters with the enemy in Poland in early August the division only claimed limited successful engagements. Although that figure was soon to rise during the first week of battle, German losses were kept to a minimum but the strength of the combat divisions was down to only 2,325 men.

On 11 August, as Russian forces fought on the upper Vistula between Army Group Centre and Army Group North, what was left of the 4th Panzer Division were hurriedly transferred to the Kurland Peninsula for another defensive battle. In Poland the situation had become much grimmer for the Germans as the Soviets moved on Warsaw. The 4th, 2nd and 9th Armies were engaged in bitter fighting as units desperately tried to hold the Vistula line from the Russians and prevent them from penetrating into Warsaw. Repeatedly, formations from other sectors of the Polish front were moved and immediately inserted into the frontal sectors to help bolster the German infantry and armoured units defending in front of Warsaw. Elements of the 19th Panzer Division were one of a number of units brought up as reinforcements. Although the Germans stiffened the defence line east of the city it did not prevent heavy combat occurring around the suburbs of Praga. It was here in these suburbs nearly five years earlier that German infantry and Panzers were victoriously fighting against Polish forces during the invasion of Poland. Now they were fighting for their lives against hardened, well-equipped and bitter Russian troops. By 14 September Praga was finally captured by the Russians, and Red Army forces now directly sent their infantry and armour across the river and held considerable stretches of the riverfront. Undeterred by the Soviets the *Panzerwaffe* remained holding tenaciously the ground west of the capital and fought for every foot. A mass of infantry, mixed with the remnants of naval and Luftwaffe groups, supported the motorised columns, as they fought against innumerable numbers of Russian tanks. Many of the German armoured vehicles were festooned with camouflage, and wherever possible moved under the cover of trees, or the cover of night to avoid being attacked by the Red Army Air Force, which had almost total control of the air on the Eastern Front.

By September 1944 the whole position in Poland was on the point of disintegration. Action in Poland had been a grueling battle of attrition for those German units that had managed to escape from the slaughter. Fortunately for the surviving German forces, the Soviet offensive had now run out of momentum. The Red Army's troops were too exhausted, and their armoured vehicles were in great need of maintenance and repair. It seemed the Germans were spared from being driven out of Poland for the time being.

A Panzer commander stands inside the cupola of his tank during the winter of 1943. The black Panzer uniform itself was made of high quality black wool, which was smooth and free of imperfections. The uniform comprised of a short black double-breasted jacket worn with loose fitting black trousers. The deeply double-breasted jacket was high waisted and was specially designed to allow the wearer to move around inside his often cramped vehicle with relative comfort. The trousers were designed to be loose also in order to allow the wearer plenty of movement.

A knocked out PzKpfw IV in the snow. This tank has more than likely been hit by an anti-tank shell to the side of the vehicle and as a result the impact has blown part of the track off. Other damage is also visible along the side of the tank.

A Tiger I moves along a snow-covered road bound for the front line. This vehicle is well camouflaged with a good overall application of winter whitewash paint. Track links have been bolted to the front of the tank for additional armoured protection.

A Hummel being prepared to be shipped out to the Eastern Front. The Hummel were issued to the heavy batteries of the Panzer artillery regiments and first saw action at Kursk in 1943. They were used successfully in Russia but were replaced in mid-1944 by tank destroyers.

In the thick snow a member of a 15cm Hummel gun crew uses a field telephone to call the fire control centre. The Hummel, which has received a full coating of winter whitewash paint is marked with the letter 'G', which denotes the gun's place within the battery.

A Panther has halted in the snow. In the distance Panzergrenadiers wearing their familiar
white camouflage smocks can be seen standing with a Tiger I.

Three StuG III Ausf G take up positions on the open steppe during winter operations in 1944. Note that two of the assault guns
have their side-skirts missing, these often being torn off during combat. The farthest assault gun appears to retain all its skirting.

A number of Panzerwerfer and a munitions vehicle can be seen during a lull in the fighting in 1944. The vehicles are preparing for a firing mission during defensive operations in the east. These multi-barrelled rocket launchers could fire simultaneously 10 15cm rockets, and cause extensive damage to the enemy front lines.

This photograph shows a StuG III Ausf G assault gun in the thick of battle. This vehicle is armed with a 7.5cm StuK 40 L/48 cannon, which both necessitated modification of the frontal superstructure and increased the overall weight to 21.3 tons.

Hitler inspects a column of PzKpfw 38 (t) Hetzer on 20 April 1944 in the Klessheim area. Accompanying the Führer that day was Keitel, Goering and Karl Otto Saur (department head of the Armaments Ministry).

Panzergrenadiers march across the vast open steppe in the wake of a Tiger I. By the winter of 1944 both the Wehrmacht and Waffen-SS had adopted a decidedly defensive posture. Note the grenadier with bayonet attached to his bolt-action rifle, suggesting that he anticipates close-quarter combat of some kind.

An impressive column of PzKpfw IV's advance through the snow with grenadiers atop,
all wearing full camouflage smocks and white-washed helmets.

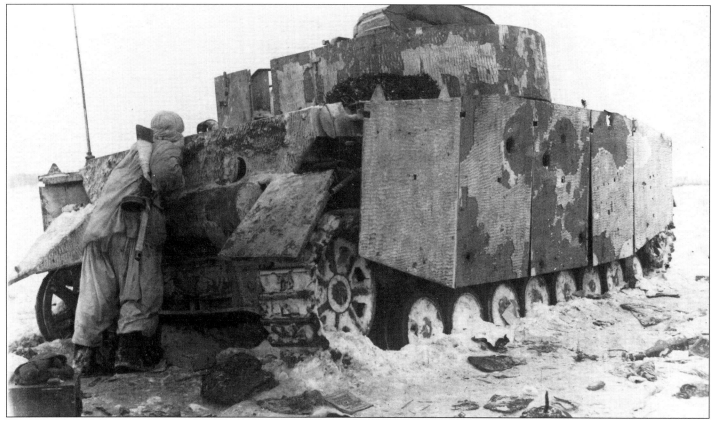

A grenadier takes cover behind a knocked out late variant PzKpfw IV during winter operations in 1944. It is evident
from the number of shell holes in the tank's side skirts that it has been embroiled in a heavy contact with the enemy.
The vehicle has probably had an internal fire as much of the Zimmerit and whitewash paint can be seen burnt off.

Here a German artillery regiment can be seen loading their artillery and halftracks on special flatbed railway cars destined for another part of the Eastern Front. In order for these transport wagons to be moved by train, special loading platforms had to be constructed. This allowed loads to be entrained and detrained quickly.

A halftrack towing supplies across a muddy field. By 1944 supplies for the *Panzerwaffe* were drastically dwindling, despite the upturn in tank production.

A crewman poses for the camera in his PzKpfw IV Ausf G command tank. Note the Zimmerit anti-magnetic mine paste on the superstructure. The vehicle has received a coating of dark yellow over sprayed with patches of olive-green and red-brown.

Moving steadily west grenadiers hitch a lift onboard an artillery tractor. Mounted on the back of the SdKfz 10/4 halftrack is a 2cm flak gun. The vehicle is towing an Sd.Ah.51 ammunition trailer.

An Elefant tank destroyer stationary on a road with its crew during operations in the later stages of the war. The vehicle carries a very interesting camouflage pattern of dark yellow with red brown and olive green wavy lines.

A Tiger tank carrying a full application of Zimmerit anti-magnetic mine paste wading across a river. This vehicle belongs to schwere Panzer Abteilung 506. In May 1943 schwere Panzer Abteilung 506 was formed and saw action alongside the 9th Panzer-Division. Within a year it had suffered heavily from continuous combat in Army Group North Ukraine.

A photograph taken the moment a Wespe self-propelled gun fires one of its 10.5cm shells at an enemy target. Although these self-propelled guns were scoring sizable successes in Russia, by mid-1944 the Allied bombing campaign were causing severe problems, and shortages of fuel and spare parts were beginning to cripple the *Panzerwaffe*. By the end of the war only a handful of Wespe machines were captured intact.

During a lull in the fighting artillerymen take a much needed rest beside their 10.5cm artillery gun during operations in the summer of 1944. It was primarily the artillery regiments that were given the task of destroying enemy positions and conducting counter-battery fire prior to an armoured assault. [Michael Cremin]

An SdKfz 250 with a full complement of troops negotiates a gradient after it has apparently crossed a railway line. A company commander raises his hand, warning the vehicle to halt. In the distance other armoured vehicles can be seen driving through a harvested wheat field. [Michael Cremin]

Two officers confer with each other whilst in the background an SdKfz 251/9 armed with the deadly short barreled 7.5cm KwK 37 L/24 is directed towards some trees. Dismounted Panzergrenadiers can be seen on foot following another SdKfz 251 through a hedgerow. Panzergrenadiers were the motorized infantry and generally travelled by motor vehicle than on foot. These troops were always moved into the thick of battle and provided armour with valuable support. [Michael Cremin]

A well dug-in Jagdpanzer 38 (t) Hetzer tank destroyer has been camouflaged by applying brushwood and vegetation over much of the vehicle. By 1944 it was imperative for armoured crews to reduce the risk of being attacked by heavily camouflaging their vehicles.

Panzergrenadiers march past a Panther. During the last two years of the war the number of Panzergrenadier divisions grew and they earned the respect of being called the Panzer Elite. With mounting losses of men and armour, the Panzergrenadiers displayed outstanding ability and endurance in the face of overwhelming odds. [Michael Cremin]

Two photographs showing the same Panther during operations on the Eastern Front in the summer of 1944. During 1944 Panthers appeared in increasing numbers on the front lines. By June 1944, Panthers were about one-half of the German tank strength both in the east and the west. [Michael Cremin]

A line of PzKpfw IV's off the production line and preparing to be shipped out to the Eastern Front to help bolster the *Panzerwaffe*. Later variants (especially Ausf H and J) were used extensively both in an offensive and defensive role.

A group of StuG III's parked in a village somewhere in Russia in 1944. Despite the StuG's proven tank-killing potential and its service on the battlefield, the vehicle gradually deprived the infantry of the vital fire support for which the assault gun was originally built, in order to supplement the massive losses in the *Panzerwaffe*.

In southern Russia a column of withdrawing StuG III Ausf F/8s rumble along a road passing Russian peasants. Despite dogged resistance in the south the *Panzerwaffe* lacked reinforcements and began to steadily dwindle. As further losses multiplied armour which had not been destroyed or encircled was forced to withdraw.

Here a Sturmpanzer IV Brummbär is parked ready for deployment in the summer of 1944. The Brummbär or 'grizzly bear' as it was nicknamed, mounted the powerful sIG 15cm gun. In early August 1944 10 Sturmpanzers were transferred to Army Group Centre to assist in suppressing the Warsaw uprising.

Waffen-SS grenadiers carrying a variety of weapons pass a stationary Panther Ausf G during operations in 1944. Note the machine gunner armed with the MG42. Behind him is a soldier carrying an MP44 assault rifle.

The PzKpfw IV played a prominent role stemming the Soviet onslaught. Despite inferior numbers, the tank performed well in defensive operations, and achieved resounding success with the elite Waffen-SS divisions.

PART III

The End

Fighting for Survival

The lull in Poland was not mirrored elsewhere on the Eastern Front. In mid-July 1944, another massive offensive was launched by the Soviet Ukrainian Fronts. On 20 August, the 2nd Ukrainian Front broke through powerful German defences supported by heavy armour, and the Red Army reached the Bulgarian border on 1 September. Within a week, Soviet troops reached the Yugoslav frontier. On 8 September, Bulgaria and Romania then declared war on Germany. Two weeks later on 23 September, Soviet forces arrived on the Hungarian border and immediately raced through the country for the Danube, finally reaching the river to the south of Budapest.

Hitler placed the utmost importance on the defence of Hungary and ordered that his premier Waffen-SS divisions, including those vital forces positioned along the Vistula in Poland should be transferred to Hungary.

Whilst IV SS Panzer Corps and two Panzergrenadier divisions were transferred to Army Group South to relieve Budapest, the *Panzerwaffe* continued to rigidly commit everything it still had. Despite the dogged resistance of many of the tank crews and supporting troops, there was no coherent strategy, and any local counter-offensives were often blunted with severe losses. The Soviets possessed too many tanks, anti-tank guns and aircraft for the Panzers and they remained incapable of causing any serious losses or delay. Little in the way of reinforcements reached them, and those that were left holding a defensive position had already been forced into various *ad-hoc* Panzer divisions that were simply thrown together with a handful of tanks and Panzergrenadiers. Much of these hastily formed formations were short-lived. The majority were either completely decimated in the fighting or had received such a mauling in battle they were reorganised into a different *ad-hoc* formation under a new commander.

For the *Panzerwaffe* fighting for survival on the Eastern Front shortages of every kind were affecting most of the old and experienced Panzer divisions. The Soviets had unmatchable material superiority, and yet, despite this major drawback, in late 1944 armoured vehicle production, including tanks, assault guns and self-propelled assault guns, was higher than in any month before May 1944. In October and November 1944 assembly plants managed to turn out 12,000 trucks by rebuilding disabled vehicles and transporting them both to the Eastern and Western Fronts. Truck strengths, especially those authorised for Panzer and Panzergrenadier divisions, were already critically low. By the end of the year the problem had become so bad that it was proposing mounting the Panzergrendiers on bicycles.

In a drastic attempt to sustain Germany's combat strength the Panzer brigades had two battalions, and Panzerjäger brigades with one battalion. But despite these fervent efforts to increase the combat strength of the *Panzerwaffe*, Panzer units and individuals of Panzer and Panzergrenadier divisions were too exhausted to avert the situation decisively. As a result the Russians continued pushing forward whilst German forces retreated through Poland to East Prussia. Along the Baltic coast, too, Soviet forces advanced, crushing those German units from all that remained of the once-mighty Army Group North. Hitler refused to allow the evacuation of 20 divisions – half a million men – which had been bypassed in the Kurland peninsula. These heavy attacks eventually cut the vast territory formerly occupied by Germany in the northeast to a few small pockets of land surrounding three ports: Libau in Kurland, Pillau in East Prussia and Danzig at the mouth of the Vistula. Here along the Baltic German defenders were reorganized as Army Group Centre in East Prussia and Army Group Kurland, the former Army Group North. All the German forces were understrength, and their defensive capabilities depended greatly on the old Prussian and Silesian fortresses of Breslau, Stettin, Küstrin, Insterburg and Königsberg.

Massive though the Soviet force was in the Baltic, it was nothing compared to the forces available to the Red Army further south. There the winter offensive was to be a massive two-pronged attack through the rest of Poland, one leading along the Warsaw – Berlin axis commanded by Zhukov, with the other for Breslau under the command of General Konev. On 12 January 1945, the Eastern Front erupted with a massive advance as Konev's offensive began with the 1st Ukrainian Front making deep wide-sweeping penetrations against hard-pressed German formations. The Russian offensive was delivered with so much weight and fury never before experienced on the Eastern Front. On the first day of the offensive the 4th Panzer Army took the full brunt of an artillery barrage followed by an armoured attack by the 1st Byelorussian Front. It had total numerical superiority over the Germans with 7 to 1 in armour alone. The vast tide of the Red Army soon swallowed up the battlefield and by the end of the first day of the new offensive it had torn a huge breach over 20 miles wide in the Vistula front. The 4th Panzer Army had almost ceased to exist. Krakow was immediately threatened and German forces quickly manoeuvred to defend this ancient city.

On 14 January, Zhukov's 1st Belorrussian Front began its long awaited drive along the Warsaw-Berlin axis, striking out from the Vistula south of Warsaw. The city was quickly encircled and fell three days later. The frozen ground ensured rapid movement for the Russian tank crews, but in some areas these massive advances were halted for a time by the skilful dispositions of the *Panzerwaffe*. Determinedly they held out in small groups of grenadiers supported by Panzers, until they too were annihilated or forced to fall back. What forces were available to try and stem the Red Army's advance to the frontiers of the Reich were pulled together into a new army group, 'Army Group Vistula'. Army Group Vistula was positioned behind the threatened front and consisted mainly of *Volkssturm* units and militia groups too young or old to serve in the regular army. Along this weak front, a number of volunteer SS units and *ad-hoc* Panzer formations bolstered the understrength and under-trained forces, but they too had little with which to impede the Russian onslaught.

Over the next few days nothing could prevent the Soviet advance. On 25 January the Russians stood in front of Breslau and two days later the city of Memel fell. As German forces continued to fall back, they tried frantically to prevent the Red Army from bursting across the borders of the Reich and onto the River Oder, which was no more than 50-miles from the Reich capital, Berlin.

The end of the *Panzerwaffe*

By early February 1945 German forces in the East had been driven back to the River Oder, the last bastion of defence before Berlin. Only three weeks earlier, the Eastern Front was still deep in Poland. Now Upper Silesia was lost; in East Prussia German forces were smashed to pieces; West Prussia and Pomerania were being defended by depleted troops thrown together, and the defence of the Oder was now being entrusted to exhausted armies that had been fighting defensive actions for months in Poland along the Vistula. What was left of these forces were supposed to hold the Oder front and fight to the death.

Along 200-miles of the defensive front the remaining Panzer divisions had no more than 70 tanks strung out along the front lines and were almost totally unprotected. A report noted that each division had to hold a frontage of approximately 20 miles. For every one mile of front some remaining regiments had one artillery piece, one heavy machine gun, two light machine guns and about 150 men. On every two and a half miles of front they had, in addition, one anti-tank gun. On every four miles they had one Panzer, and on every six miles one battalion. They were confronted by an enemy force made up of three tank armies consisting of thousands of tanks. Against this massive Soviet force was the German 9th, 4th Panzer and 17th Armies that fielded some 400,000 troops, 4,100 artillery pieces and 1,150 tanks. The First Byelorussian and First Ukrainian Fronts had the Germans outnumbered on the average by 10:1 in tanks and self-propelled artillery, 9:1 in artillery and troops. In the First Byelorussian Front alone this Russian Army had more infantry, tanks and artillery than the entire German Army on the Eastern Front.

In spite of the overwhelming superiority German forces prepared their defensive positions along the Oder. On the night of 14 February the 11th SS Panzer Army actually mounted an attack, code-named 'Sonnenwende', and hit weak Russian units with its tanks. Although the daring Panzer attack caught the Russians by surprise, 'Sonnenwende' was no more than a reprieve for the Germans. Along whole areas of the front the once-proud Panzer divisions had been reduced to skeletal formations on a stricken field. They were now not only vastly outnumbered but seriously lacked fuel supplies, lubricants and ammunition. When parts of the front caved in armoured formations were often forced to destroy their equipment, so nothing was left for the conquering enemy. The Germans no longer had the manpower, war plant or transportation to accomplish a proper build-up of forces on the Oder. Commanders could do little to compensate for the deficiencies, and in many sectors of the front they did not have any coherent planning in the event the defence of the river failed.

When the Russians successfully attacked the Oder in mid-April 1945, the hodgepodge force of what was left of the German Army fought out in desperation as the Soviet thrust carved its way across the river, capturing the town of Kustrin, and heading towards the Nazi capital.

As the Russians poured through along the Berlin highway the III SS Panzer Corps were given the task of scraping together enough armoured vehicles to defend the line on the 3rd Panzer Army's flank along the Finow Canal. North of the Canal stood the 4th SS Police Division, the 5th Jäger Division, and the 25th Panzer Grenadier Division. Standing to the east of Berlin was the LVI Panzer Corps. Although these German formations fought bitterly to defend the capital from the advancing Red Army, by 24 April the Russians systematically completed the great encirclement of steel and fire around Berlin. The battle of Berlin was doomed, but even during the battle the commander of the 503rd Heavy Tank Battalion was able to report on 26 April, that he still had six tanks ready for active service in the defence of the routes leading into Berlin. This was hardly enough tanks to stem the mighty Red Army, but even so courageous Tiger crews fought on ceaselessly trying to prolong the death throes of the *Panzerwaffe*.

During the last days of the war most of the remaining Panzer divisions continued to fight as a unit until they destroyed their equipment and surrendered. Amongst the last Panzer divisions of the war was formed Panzer Division 'Clausewitz', with two battalions of two tank companies each with a total of 56 tanks and assault guns. Although it saw extensive action, its success was limited and localized and did nothing to avert enemy successes. At the time of surrender, the combined strength of the entire *Panzerwaffe* was 2,023 tanks, 738 assault guns and 159 Flakpanzers. Surprisingly this was the same strength that was used to attack Russia in 1941. But the size of the German Army in 1945 was not the same; it was far too inadequate in strength for any type of task. Although the war had ended, the *Panzerwaffe* still existed, but not as the offensive weapon it had been in the early Blitzkrieg years.

Nobody could deny that the men of the *Panzerwaffe*, in their brief and extraordinary existence, had won a reputation for daring and professionalism in combat. Despite the titanic struggles which had been placed upon them during the war in Russia the *Panzerwaffe* provided the very backbone of Germany's defence. Although its strength never exceeded one-fifth of that of the German Army, its crews fought with courage and zeal to the end.

A completely destroyed PzKpfw IV stands twisted next to a charred tree. This Panzer has evidently suffered a violent explosion on board with its turret virtually blown off. Amazingly the vehicle's tracks are still intact.

An assault gun crew pose for the camera in front of their late variant StuG III. All the crew are distinctively wearing the Sturmartillerie uniform. The uniform was made entirely of field-grey cloth. The collar patches consisted of the death's head emblems, which were stitched on patches of dark blue-green cloth and were edged with bright red Waffenfarbe piping. However, officers did not display the death head collar patches, but wore the field service collar patches instead. No piping on the collar patches was used.

An interesting photograph showing a crewman posing for the camera in front of his PzKpfw IV Ausf G command tank in the summer of 1944. Note the coating of Zimmerit plaster coating on the vehicle, and the spaced armour plates around the turret, plus the star antenna.

Six photographs taken in sequence showing Panthers moving along a dusty road during operations in the early autumn of 1944. During the bitter fighting in Poland the Panther was used extensively to blunt the weight of the Russian drive. As German troops found themselves constantly becoming either encircled or cut-off the Panthers were organized into special rescue units to come to their comrades' relief. During the course of these daring rescue missions Panther crews fought with tenacity and courage, but time and time again the sheer weight of the Soviet army overwhelmed them. Although many Panthers were lost in action as a result of these rescue missions, it was the lack of fuel and ammunition that eventually forced these lethal machines to a standstill.

A column of vehicles including halftracks have halted on a dirt road west of the Vistula in the summer of 1944. Having advanced into the heart of Poland the Red Army began planning their final offensive into Germany and on to Berlin.

A stationary Hummel. This heavy self-propelled gun carried just eighteen 15cm rounds, but was a potent weapon against Soviet armour.

Two photographs showing the same Panther Ausf G during operations on the Eastern Front in autumn 1944. The improved Ausf G had improved new vision devices and thicker side armour. Some of them had all-steel road wheels and a number had an early infrared sighting device – technology that was well ahead of its time.

A Hummel on the move to join its battery during defensive operations in the east. This vehicle can clearly be seen carrying a number of various provisions under the 15cm gun on the frontal deck, including rolled up canvas sheeting used to help protect the crew against the weather.

A Hummel undergoing maintenance at a workshop in Poland in the summer of 1944. A crewmember can be seen in the driver`s compartment.

Panthers being paraded before their departure to the Eastern Front in 1944. During the last months of the war few Panthers were left intact to the engage the enemy as it thundered towards the Reich capital.

A Panther crew is preparing to change tracks for cross-country combat operations. The Panther tracks were fitted with chevroned cleats intended to increase traction and reduce slipping on icy conditions and on hard surfaces such as concrete and cobblestones.

The crew of a late production Tiger scours the terrain a head trying to deduce the location of the advancing enemy. By 1944 the Red Army had developed 100mm and 152mm guns that could destroy the Tiger. By the end of the war, other tanks had been developed that outclassed the Tiger – the Joseph Stalin II was among them.

A Panther has halted on a road during operations in Poland in the late summer of 1944. The continuous fighting in the east gradually took their toll on tracks and other moving parts of the Panther, and those that were left fought a desperate defensive action all the way into Germany.

Panthers have been loaded for transport to the East in 1944 to meet the ever-growing threat of the Russian advance. By this period of the war rail transport was very hazardous and generally tanks were interspersed with divisional transport to minimize the risk from aerial attack. However, in this photograph no precautions have been taken.

A Tiger rumbles along a road during the autumn of 1944. Track links have been bolted to the front of the tank for additional armoured protection.

Two PzKpfw IV Ausf H move across open ground followed by an SdKfz 251 Ausf C. The commander in the tank leading the armoured column scours the rolling countryside for any signs of enemy movement.

A grenadier armed with an MP40 approaches a stationary StuG III Ausf G, which is already laden with troops. Note the letter `A` painted in red or yellow on the rear superstructure plate indicating the position of the vehicle in the gun battery.

A destroyed PzKpfw IV on the Eastern Front during the winter of 1944/45. The vehicle appears
to have received a direct hit and as a consequence of the shell's impact it has blown off most of
the side-skirts. A thick coating of Zimmerit is evident over the chassis and turret

An SdKfz 251 is towing a support vehicle across a stream during autumn operations in Hungary in 1945.
These vehicles belong to the 24th Panzer Division, which had had seen extensive fighting in Russia.

On board a flatbed railway car is a Hummel destined for the front lines in the East. Five of the six-man crew poses for the camera with their vehicle's potent 15cm gun. By late 1944, virtually all the Hummels had been lost in action or were simply abandoned by the crews when they run out of fuel.

Polish soldiers examine a captured Nashorn in early 1945. Branches from trees have been applied to the side of the vehicle in order to try and conceal it from enemy observation. The high profile of the Nashorn made it hard to conceal, but its long-range gun enabled it to fight at more extreme ranges than other tank destroyers.

An abandoned TigerII in the spring of 1945. This massive tank was introduced in the ranks of the *Panzerwaffe* in early 1944. It had a powerful 8.8cm KwK 43 gun with a barrel over 20ft in length, whilst the rounds weighed some 20kgs.

A knocked out Panther stands on a road somewhere in eastern Germany in the spring of 1945. The success of the Panther undoubtedly helped changed the fortunes of the *Panzerwaffe* in Russia, albeit only temporarily.

An interesting photograph showing a column of StuG III`s during the winter of 1944/45. To maintain their speed, the accompanying infantry were carried on the tanks and other armoured vehicles. When they ran into stiff opposition, they immediately dismounted to avoid suffering heavy casualties. [Michael Cremin]

Pieces of foliage have been applied to this whitewashed Hummel in Poland during the winter of 1944/45. By this period of the war much of the burden had fallen on the assault artillery and tank destroyer battalions to try and stem the Red Army onslaught. [Michael Cremin]

An SdKfz 251 makes its way through a village during intensive heavy fighting in western Poland in 1944/45. The SdKfz 251 had become not just a halftrack intended to simply transport infantry to the edge of the battlefield, but also a fully-fledged fighting vehicle. [Michael Cremin]

An SdKfz 10 advances through a destroyed village. This vehicle mounts a shielded 2cm Flak 30. Note the magazine containers on the drop sides. By 1944 both Wehrmacht and Waffen-SS mechanized formations were well-equipped with flak guns.

Two crewmembers can be seen inside an SdKfz 250 during operations in Poland in late 1944. This whitewashed vehicle is armed with an MG34 machine gun with splinter shield.

Three photographs showing abandoned Jagdpanzer IV`s. With a drastic need for new armoured fighting vehicles, more second generation tank destroyers were built.  One such vehicle that came off the production line in 1944 was the Jagdpanzer IV. This vehicle, built on the chassis of a PzKpfw IV, weighed 28.5 tons and was nicknamed `Guderian's duck`. The vehicle was equal to any enemy tanks thanks to its potent 7.5cm gun. The Jagdpanzer saw extensive service in the east and with its reliability and well-sloped thick frontal armour it became a highly efficient fighting vehicle, if only for a short period of time.

Another abandoned Jagdpanzer IV armed with the PaK 39 L/48. Note the engine doors at the rear of the vehicle are open showing the fans for the powerful Maybach HL120 TRM engine.

A knocked out Tiger I east of Berlin in April 1945. This Tiger may possibly be from the SS schwere Panzer Abteilung 503 which fought in this area against the advancing Red Army.

Two photographs showing abandoned StuG III`s in the early spring of 1945. During the last two years of the war the StuG was gradually called upon for offensive and defensive fire support, where it was gradually embroiled in an anti-tank role trying to stem the might of the Red Army. During the last weeks of the war as fuel and spare parts became scarce many StuG`s were either destroyed or simply abandoned by the crews.

APPENDIX I

The Panzer Reconnaissance Battalion, mid-1943

Battalion Headquarters (5 Officers, 22 men)
Communications Platoon (1 Officer, 60 men)
Train and Maintenance (6 Officers, 87 men)
Heavy Armoured Car Platoon (1 Officer, 21 men)

Heavy Company (5 Officers and 199 men)
Company HQ (1 Officer, 15 men)
Antitank Platoon (1 Officer, 36 men)
Infantry Gun Platoon (1 Officer, 24 men)
Pioneer Platoon (1 Officer, 58 men)
Cannon Platoon (1 Officer, 37 men)
Company Train and Maintenance (29 men)

Armoured Car Company (4 Officers and 114 men)
Company Headquarters (1 Officer, 9 men)
Heavy Platoon (2 Officers, 22 men)
Three Light Platoons, each (1 Officer or NCO, 17 men)
Train and Maintenance (30 men)

Armoured Car Company (3 Officers, 110 men)
Company Headquarters (1 Officer, 10 men)
Four Platoons, each (1 Officer or NCO, 17 men)
Train and Maintenance (30 men)

Light Column (1 Officer, 50 men)
Column HQ (1 Officer, 14 men)
Detachment (11 men)
Two Detachments, each (9 men)
Train (7 men)

Two Light Armoured Rifle Companies (3 Officers, 233 men), each comprised of:
Company Headquarters (1 Officer, 12 men)
Train and Maintenance (30 men)

Heavy Platoon comprised of:
Platoon HQ (1 Officer, 5 men)
Mortar Group (18 men)
Two Heavy Machine Gun Groups, each (17 men)

Three Rifle Platoons, each comprised of:
Platoon HQ (1 Officer or NCO, 8 men)
Three Rifle Squads, each comprised of 12 men

Total strength of 1161 all ranks (32 Officers and 1129 men)

The Panzer Reconnaissance Battalion, mid-1944

Battalion Headquarters (4 Officers, 18 men)

Staff Company (3 Officers, 113 men)
Company HQ (1 Officer, 11 men)
Communications Platoon (1 Officer, 43 men)
Two Heavy Armoured Car Platoons, *each* (1 Officer *or* NCO, 23 men)
Cannon Group (12 men)

Supply Company (7 Officers, 202 men)
Company HQ (2 Officers, 16 men)
Medical Detachment (1 Officer, 4 men)
Maintenance Detachment (3 Officers, 112 men)
Fuel Detachment (16 men)
Munitions Detachment (13 men)
Supply Detachment (1 Officer, 41 men)

Heavy Company (4 Officers, 150 men)
Company HQ (1 Officer, 14 men)
Cannon Platoon (1 Officer, 31 men)
Pioneer Platoon (1 Officer, 50 men)
8 cm Mortar Platoon (1 Officer, 55 men)

Armoured Car Company (3 Officers, 82 men)
Company HQ (1 Officer, 12 men)
Four Platoons, *each* (1 Officer *or* NCO, 17 men)

Light Reconnaissance Company (3 Officers, 164 men)
Company HQ (1 Officer, 17 men)
Mortar Group (17 men)
Cannon Group (9 men)
Three Rifle Platoons, *each* comprised of:
Platoon HQ (1 Officer *or* NCO, 4 men)
Three Rifle Squads, each comprised of 12 men

Heavy Reconnaissance Company (3 Officers, 180 men):
Company HQ (1 Officer, 17 men)
Heavy Platoon comprised of:
Platoon HQ (1 Officer, 8 men)
Mortar Group (15 men)

Cannon Group (8 men)
Two Heavy Machine Gun Groups, *each* (11 men)
Three Rifle Platoons, *each* comprised of:
Platoon HQ (1 Officer *or* NCO, 6 men)
Three Rifle Squads, each comprised of 10 men
Total strength of 936 all ranks (23 Officers and 913 men)

Armoured Composition of the Battalion

Heavy Armoured Car Platoon
Now part of the HQ Company with each Platoon fielding six SdKfz 234/1 heavy armoured cars, some of which mounted either a 5cm gun or 7.5cm Pak 40.

Cannon Group
Consisted of three SdKfz 234/3, mounting the 7.5 cm cannon.

Pioneer Platoon
Its three Squads were fifteen strong and were transported in two SdKfz 251/7 pioneer halftracks.

8 cm Mortar Platoon
Had six SdKfz 251/2 halftracks, each mounting an 8 cm mortar, with an additional SdKfz 251 for Platoon HQ.

Armoured Car Company
Equipped with three SdKfz 231 and three SdKfz 232 vehicles, again eight wheeled, each with a four man crew. The three Light Platoons used four SdKfz 222 and two SdKfz 223 armoured cars.

The Rifle Company
This Company operated the SdKfz 250 halftrack with a squad of twelve men and a leader and assistant. Both vehicles carried their own machine pistol and light machine gun.

The Mortar Group
Two SdKfz 250/8 and a 250/1 for munitions.

The Panzer Grenadier Battalion, 1943

Battalion Headquarters (5 Officers, 16 men)
Communications Platoon (24 men)
Battalion Train and Maintenance (5 Officers, 60 men)

Heavy Company (5 Officers, 199 men)
Company HQ (1 Officer, 15 men)
Antitank Platoon (1 Officer, 36 men)
Infantry Gun Platoon (1 Officer, 24 men)
Pioneer Platoon (1 Officer, 58 men)
Cannon Platoon (1 Officer, 37 men)
Company Train and Maintenance (29 men)

Three Rifle Companies (4 Officers, 223 men), *each* **comprised of:**
Company HQ (1 Officer, 13 men)
Company Train and Maintenance (25 men)
Heavy Platoon comprised of:
Platoon HQ (1 Officer, 12 men)
Mortar Group (16 men)
Cannon Group (8 men)
Two Heavy Machine Gun Groups, *each* (11 men)
Three Rifle Platoons, *each* comprised of:
Platoon HQ (1 Officer *or* NCO, 6 men)
Three Rifle Squads, each comprised of 12 men
Total strength of 995 all ranks (27 Officers and 968 men)

Armoured Composition of the Battalion

Battalion Headquarters
Comprised of the command staff of the Battalion with two halftracks, plus a number of field cars and motorcycles.

Communications Platoon
Consisted of a variety of vehicles for maintaining radio and line communications within the Battalion.

Anti-tank Platoon
Three SdKfz 251 halftracks, plus one SdKfz 250/1 for ammunition were used in a typical Panzer Grenadier Battalion. These were authorized to tow three 5 cm Pak in its Anti-tank Platoon, but also the 3.7cm Pak. The lethal 7.5cm Pak 40 also found its way into the Anti-tank platoon during 1943.

Infantry Gun Platoon
Three SdKfz 251/4 halftracks towed 7.5cm infantry guns and also acted as ammunition carriers. There was an SdKfz 251 at HQ.

Cannon Platoon
This fielded six self-propelled 7.5 cm guns, each mounted on an SdKfz 251/9 armoured halftrack, plus an HQ vehicle and ammunition carrier.

Pioneer Platoon
This consisted of three Squads, each fifteen strong with two light machine guns and carried in two SdKfz 251/7 armoured halftracks. Platoon HQ was supported by an SdKfz 251/10 with 3.7 cm gun and a additional vehicle comprising of flamethrower equipment.

Heavy Anti-tank Rifle Platoon
This Anti-tank Rifle Platoon consisted of SdKfz 250/11 halftracks towing the 2.8 cm sPzB 41 anti-tank rifle.

The Rifle Company
Comprised of SdKfz 251/1 armoured halftracks carrying two gun teams, each with a gunner and loader, and four riflemen.

Heavy Platoon
Consisted of SdKfz 251/2 armoured halftracks which were armed with 8cm mortars that were fired from the vehicle.

Platoon Headquarters
The Platoon Headquarters comprised of an SdKfz 251/9 or 10, which mounted its own 3.7cm Pak in place of a light machine gun. On some of the vehicles the 7.5cm infantry guns were mounted.

Company HQ
Was equipped with two SdKfz 251/3 command halftracks.

APPENDIX IV

The Panzer Grenadier Battalion, late 1943

Battalion Headquarters (6 Officers, 20 men)
Communications Platoon (1 Officer, 22 men)
Battalion Train and Maintenance (4 Officers, 77 men)

Heavy Company (4 Officers, 133 men)
Company HQ (1 Officer, 16 men)
Antitank Platoon (1 Officer, 31 men)
Infantry Gun Platoon (1 Officer, 24 men)
Cannon Platoon (1 Officer, 34 men)
Company Train and Maintenance (28 men)

Three Rifle Companies (3 Officers, 217 men), *each*
comprised of:
Company HQ (1 Officer, 27 men)
Company Train and Maintenance (25 men)
Heavy Platoon comprised of:
Platoon HQ (1 Officer, 10 men)
Mortar Group (15 men)
Cannon Group (8 men)
Two Heavy Machine Gun Groups, *each* (11 men)
Three Rifle Platoons, *each* comprised of:
Platoon HQ (1 Officer *or* NCO, 6 men)
Three Rifle Squads, each comprised of 10 men

Total strength of 927 all ranks (24 Officers and 903 men)

The Panzer Grenadier Battalion, 1944

Battalion Headquarters (4 Officers, 16 men)
Communications Platoon (1 Officer, 22 men)

Supply Company (7 Officers, 156 men)
Company HQ (2 Officers, 11 men)
Medical Detachment (1 Officer, 4 men)
Maintenance Detachment (3 Officers, 79 men)
Fuel Detachment (12 men)
Munitions Detachment (14 men)
Supply Detachment (1 Officer, 36 men)

Heavy Company (3 Officers, 94 men)
Company HQ (1 Officer, 18 men)
Cannon Platoon (1 Officer, 31 men)
12 cm Mortar Platoon (1 Officer, 45 men)

Three Rifle Companies (3 Officers, 180 men), *each* **comprised of:**
Company HQ (1 Officer, 17 men)
Heavy Platoon comprised of:
Platoon HQ (1 Officer, 8 men)
Mortar Group (15 men)
Cannon Group (8 men)
Two Heavy Machine Gun Groups, *each* (11 men)
Three Rifle Platoons, *each* comprised of:
Platoon HQ (1 Officer *or* NCO, 6 men)
Three Rifle Squads, each comprised of 10 men

Total strength of 852 all ranks (24 Officers and 828 men)

Armoured Composition of the Battalion

Anti-tank Platoon
Three SdKfz 251/17 halftracks, some mounting the 2 cm anti-aircraft gun.

12 cm Mortar Platoon
Comprised of SdKfz 251/1, but the 12cm mortars were not fired from inside the vehicle. The Platoon also consisted of the SdKfz 250 ammunition carrier as well.

The Rifle Company
Consisted of a number of vehicles for transportation and for carrying various equipment and ammunition. During late 1943 each squad was armed with its own 8.8cm Panzerschreck anti-tank launcher.

Platoon HQ
Consisted of the SdKfz 251/17 armoured halftrack mounting its own 2cm Flak gun.

Heavy Platoon
Six SdKfz 251/17 models were in one Company. Towards the end of 1943 the Machine Gun Group vehicles along, with the Platoon HQ machine, were again supposedly SdKfz 251/17 models, for a total of six in the Company. Each vehicle mounted a single machine gun team and was supported by a 2cm Flak gun crew.

The Panzer Battalion circa 1943

Battalion Headquarters (8 Officers, 16 men)

Staff Company (6 Officers, 250 men[1])
Company HQ (1 Officer, 3 men)
Reconnaissance Platoon (1 Officer, 24 men)
Communication Platoon (1 Officer, 17 men)
Scout and Pioneer Platoon (1 Officer, 52 men)
Anti-aircraft Platoon (44 men)
Train and Maintenance (2 Officers, 110 men[2])

Four Companies (3 Officers, 158 men[3]) *each* **comprised of;**
Company HQ (1 Officer, 13 men[4])
Trains and Maintenance (47 men[5])
Four Platoons, *each* comprised of (1 Officer *or* NCO and 24 men)
Total strength of 924 all ranks (26 Officers and 898 men), or 1030 men (26 Officers and 1014 men) in Panther Battalion.

Armoured Composition of the Battalion

Reconnaissance Platoon
Equipped mainly with five Panzer IV or Panther tanks.

Communication Platoon
Panzer III models or Panthers with three tanks.

Scout and Pioneer Platoon
Comprised of four Motorcycle Sections, each of ten men carried on motorcycles or Kettenkrads, with a single light machine gun per Section. The three Pioneer Sections were each nine men strong, carried in an SdKfz 251/7 with a halftrack or truck for equipment.

Anti-aircraft Platoon
Various halftracks were used in the Platoon that occasionally mounted four 2cm cannons.

The Panzer Company
Equipped with twenty two tanks of either the Panzer IV or Panther type.

---

1   318 men in Panther Battalion.

2   178 men in Panther Battalion.

3   170 men in Panther Battalion.

4   15 men in Panther Battalion.

5   58 men in Panther Battalion.

APPENDIX VII

The Panzer Battalion mid -1944

Battalion Headquarters (4 Officers, 10 men)

Staff Company (3 Officers, 142 men)
Company HQ (1 Officer, 4 men)
Communication and Reconnaissance Platoon (1 Officer, 45 men)
Scout and Pioneer Platoon (1 Officer, 53 men)
Anti-aircraft Platoon (40 men)

Supply Company (7 Officers, 174 men1)
Company HQ (3 Officers, 19 men)
Medical Detachment (1 Officer, 7 men2)
Maintenance Detachment (2 Officers, 87 men3)
Fuel Detachment (12 men4)
Munitions Detachment (15 men5)
Supply Detachment (1 Officer, 34 men6)

Four Companies (3 Officers, 100 men), *each* **comprised of;**
Company HQ (1 Officer, 17 men)
Reserve Platoon (10 men)
Three Platoons, *each* comprised of (1 Officer *or* NCO and 24 men)

Total strength of 752 all ranks (26 Officers and 726 men), or 848 men (26 Officers and 822 men) in Panther Battalion.

The Panzer Company
Reduced to three tank Platoons. Each Platoon had five tanks.

---

1 270 men in Panther Battalion.
2 8 men in Panther Battalion.
3 164 men in Panther Battalion.
4 26 men in Panther Battalion.
5 18 men in Panther Battalion.
6 35 men in Panther Battalion.

Notes on Eastern Front Panzer Divisions

1. Panzer-Division

Formed October 1935 at Weimar.
Divisional Insignia:
For preparation against Russia a new symbol was designed, a yellow inverted 'Y'. However, the painting of the new divisional sign was not widely liked by the crews and the emblem was applied on leading vehicles, whilst the older style oakleaf was retained on support vehicles. From 1943–1945, the use of the white oakleaf was still seen many vehicles and was unofficially accepted by OKW.
Units:
Panzer Regiment 1
Panzer Artillery Regiment 73
Panzergrenadier Regiments 1, 113
Panzer Aufkl Abt (Reconnaissance Section) 1.
Theatres of Operation:
Northern and Central Groups Russia June 1941–February 1943
Balkans and Greece 1943
Ukraine November–December 1943
Hungary and Austria June 1944–May 1945

2. Panzer-Division

Formed October 1935 at Würzburg.
Divisional Insignia:
For the invasion of Russia the division used a new inverted 'Y' with one mark. This was used during the first two years of the campaign in Russia. During mid-1943 a white trident sign replaced this emblem. The trident was used for the remainder of the war.
Units:
Panzergrenadier Regiments 2, 304
Panzer Regiment 3
Panzer Artillery Regiment 74
Panzer Aufkl Abt (Reconnaissance) 2
Theatres of Operation:
Army Group Centre (Smolensk, Orel, Kiev) 1942–1943
France and Germany 1944–1945

3. Panzer-Division

Formed October 1935 at Berlin.
Divisional Insignia:
For the invasion of Russia a new sign was introduced and was regarded as the official sign. It was an inverted yellow 'Y' with two marks. In spite of the new sign, units of the division could use the bear in a white shield, and the tanks in Panzer-Regiment.6 also used the standing bear without a shield. The bear was often painted in various colours that included, white, yellow, blue and red. In 1943 Panzer-Regiment 6 adopted a regimental emblem that comprised a black shield that was round on the bottom and flat on top, with the 1939-40 divisional sign of the 4. Panzer-Division, and a pair of crossed swords below this.
Units:
Panzergrenadier Regiments 3, 394
Panzer Regiment 6
Panzer Artillery Regiment 75
Panzer Aufkl Abt 3
Theatres of Operation:
Central Russia 1941–1942
Southern Russia–Kharkov and Dnepr Bend 1943
Ukraine and Poland 1944
Hungary and Austria 1944–1945

4. Panzer-Division

Formed November 1938 at Würzburg.
Divisional Insignia:
In 1941 for the Russian campaign the division used the inverted 'Y' with three marks, and used this for the remainder of the war.
Units:
Panzergrenadier Regiments 12, 33
Panzer Regiment 35
Panzer Artillery Regiment 103
Panzer Aufkl Abt 4
Theatres of Operation:
Central Russia–Caucasus 1942, Kursk 1943 and Latvia 1944
Germany 1945

5. Panzer-Division

Formed at Oppeln in November 1939.
Divisional Insignia:
On the Eastern Front Panzer-Regiment.3 1 adopted the red devil's head as a regimental symbol. This emblem, together with the yellow 'X' was used until the end of the war.
Units:
Panzergrenadier Regiments 13, 14
Panzer Regiment 31
Panzer Artillery Regiment 116
Panzer Aufkl Abt 5
Theatres of Operation:
Central Russia–Kursk, Dnepr, Latvia, and Kurland 1941–1944
East Prussia 1944–45

6. Panzer-Division

Formed at Wuppertal in October 1939.
Divisional Insignia:
For the Russian campaign it used the letter symbol 'X' in yellow. During the drive on Moscow a yellow 'war hatchet' was used as a temporary sign.
Units:
Panzergrenadier Regiments 4, 114
Panzer Regiment 11
Panzer Artillery Regiment 76
Panzer Aufkl Abt 6
Theatres of Operation:
Russia 1941–44
Hungary and Austria 1944–45

7. Panzer-Division

Formed at Weimar in October 1939.
Divisional Insignia:
For Operation *Barbarossa* the division adopted a new sign, a yellow 'Y'. The division fought continuously in Russia and retained the yellow 'Y' until the end of the war.
Units:
Panzergrenadier Regiments 6, 7
Panzer Regiment 25
Panzer Artillery Regiment 78
Panzer Aufkl Abt 7
Theatres of Operation:
Central Russia 1941
Refit in France 1942
Southern Russia 1942
Kharkov 1942
Baltic Coast and Prussia 1944–45

8. Panzer-Division

Formed at Berlin in October 1938.
Divisional Insignia:
In Russia the division used a new sign, a yellow 'Y' with one yellow mark. It was used until the end of the war.
Units:
Panzergrenadier Regiments 8, 28
Panzer Regiment 10
Panzer Artillery Regiment 80
Panzer Aufkl Abt 8
Theatres of Operation:
Southern Russia 1941
Central Russia 1942
Kursk 1943

11. Panzer-Division

Formed August 1940 at Breslau.
Divisional Insignia:
This division received the official sign of a yellow circle divided by a vertical bar. The division's personal emblem was a white-stenciled figure of a ghost brandishing a sword. Because of this emblem the division became known as the 'Ghost' division, and fought until the end of the war.
Units:
Panzergrenadier Regiments 110, 111
Panzer Regiment 15
Panzer Artillery Regiment 119
Panzer Aufkl Abt 11
Theatres of Operation:
Russia 1941–44 (Orel, Belgorod, Krivoi Rog and Korsun)
Northern France 1944

12. Panzer-Division

Formed in October 1940.
Divisional Insignia:
Its symbol was a yellow circle divided into three equal segments by 'Y'. The division did not modify its insignia and it carried it through the rest of the war.
Units:
Panzergrenadier Regiments 5, 25
Panzer Regiment 29
Panzer Artillery Regiment 2
Panzer Aufkl Abt 12
Theatres of Operation:
Russia Army Group Centre 1941–1944
Russia 1941 Minsk and Smolensk
Leningrad 1942
Orel and Middle Dnepr 1943
Kurland 1945 (captured by the Red Army)

13. Panzer-Division

Formed in October 1940.
Divisional Insignia:
This division primarily served on the Eastern Front and also in Hungary. It retained its emblem of a yellow circle divided into squares until the end of the war.
Units:
Panzergrenadier Regiments 66, 93
Panzer Regiment 4
Panzer Artillery Regiment 13
Panzer Aufkl Abt 13
Theatre of Operations:
Rumania 1941
Russia 1941–1944
Kiev 1942
Caucasus and the Kuban 1943–1944
Krivoi Rog 1944
Germany 1944
Hungary 1944–1945

14. Panzer-Division

Formed in August 1940.
Divisional Insignia:
The divisional sign was a diamond with the lower sides extended to form an 'X'.
Units:
Panzergrenadier Regiments 103, 108
Panzer Regiment 36
Panzer Artillery Regiment 4
Panzer Aufkl Abt 14
Theatres of Operation:
Southern Russia 1941
December 1942 (completely decimated at Stalingrad)

16. Panzer-Division

Formed in August 1940.
Divisional Insignia:
This divisional insignia received a 'Y' with one bar across the shaft. Its emblem was seen on the Eastern Front until it was destroyed at Stalingrad in late 1942. A new division was formed and received the same symbol. Sometimes the sign was seen outlined in black. The reason for the black marking is not really known, but it probably suggests that the division were paying their respects to the loss of the first formation.
Units:
Panzergrenadier Regiments 64, 79
Panzer Regiment 2
Panzer Artillery Regiment 16
Panzer Aufkl Abt 16
Theatres of Operation:
Southern Russia 1941

December 1942 (completely decimated at Stalingrad)
Reformed in France 1943
Russia-Kiev 1943-1945

17. Panzer-Division

Formed in October 1940.
Divisional Insignia:
This division's emblem was entirely seen on the Eastern Front and was applied with a yellow 'Y' with two bars across the shaft.
Units:
Panzergrenadier Regiments 40, 63
Panzer Regiment 39
Panzer Artillery Regiment 27
Panzer Aufkl Abt 17
Theatres of Operation:
Russia (Central and Southern Sectors) 1941–1945

18. Panzer-Division

Formed in October 1940.
Divisional Insignia:
The division's emblem was a yellow 'Y' with three bars across its shaft. Panzer- Brigade 8 had a special marking, but this was not a divisional emblem. It had a shield edged white, with a white skull and lines of water in white. The division was disbanded in 1943 and was reorganized as an artillery division, but continued using the same divisional sign.
Major Units:
Panzergrenadier Regiments 52, 101
Panzer Regiment 18
Panzer Artillery Regiment 88
Panzer Aufkl Abt 8
Theatres of Operation:
Russia (Central and Southern Sectors) 1941–1943

19. Panzer-Division

Formed in October 1940.
Divisional Insignia:
Because of the area where the division was formed it adopted a yellow wolf-trap insignia. This emblem was seen on Panzers primarily on the Eastern Front, but did serve in Poland, notably in the Warsaw uprising in August 1944.
Major Units:
Panzergrenadier Regiments 73, 74
Panzer Regiment 27
Panzer Artillery Regiment 19
Panzer Aufkl Abt 19
Theatres of Operation:
1941–1944 Russia (Central and Southern Sectors)

20. Panzer-Division

Formed in October 1940.
Divisional Insignia:
Its symbol was a yellow 'E' on its side, arms down, identical to the early 3. Panzer-Division emblem. In late 1943 the division received a new divisional insignia, which was a yellow arrow breaking through a curved borderline.
Major Units:
Panzergrenadier Regiments 59, 112
Panzer Regiment 21
Panzer Artillery Regiment 92
Panzer Aufkl Abt 20
Theatres of Operations:
Russia 1941–1944
Moscow 1941
Orel 1943
Rumania 1944
East Prussia 1944
Hungary 1944

21. Panzer-Division

Formed in the field during February 1941.
Divisional Insignia:
This emblem did vary and looked like a rectangle rather than a letter 'D'. In northern France in 1944 the new formation also used the 'D' split by the bar, which was painted either in white or yellow. Some of the markings still existed by the time it saw action in the East during the last months of the war.
Units:
Panzergrenadier Regiments 125, 192
Panzer Regiment 22
Panzer Artillery Regiment 155
Panzer Aufkl Abt 21
Theatres of Operations:
Eastern Front 1945

22. Panzer-Division

Formed in October 1941 in France.
Divisional Insignia:
The symbol of this division was a yellow arrow with two bars across the shaft. The sign made its debut on the Eastern Front in 1941. After it was almost decimated at Stalingrad the component units were distributed to 7. Panzer-Division and 23.Panzergreandier-Regiment 129.
Units:
Panzergrenadier Regiments 129, 140
Panzer Regiment 204
Panzer Artillery Regiment 140
Panzer Aufkl Abt 140

Theatres of Operations:
Russia Central Front 1942 (almost decimated at Stalingrad)

23. Panzer-Division

Formed in October 1941 in France.
Divisional Insignia:
The division adopted a personal emblem of a white silhouette of the Eiffel Tower. Often, these two signs were used together and they were seen in Russia, Poland, Hungary, and the final weeks of the war.
Units:
Panzergrenadier Regiments 126, 128
Panzer Regiment 23
Panzer Artillery Regiment 128
Panzer Aufkl Abt 23
Theatres of Operation:
Russia 1942–1944
Kharkov 1943
Stalingrad 1943
Caucasus 1943
Dnepr Bend 1944
Poland 1944 (refit)
Hungary 1944

24. Panzer-Division

Formed in February 1942.
Divisional Insignia:
Because this division was formed from the old 1.Kavallerie-Division the armoured force decided to retain its old division's history with a 'Leaping horse and rider' sign. In late 1942 the division was destroyed at Stalingrad, but was reformed in France in 1943. The new division, however, replaced the 'Leaping horse and rider' emblem with a simple bar leaping a barrier in the open circle. This was often painted in yellow.
Units:
Panzergrenadier Regiments 21, 26
Panzer Regiment 24
Panzer Artillery Regiment 89
Panzer Aufkl Abt 24
Theatres of Operation:
Russian 1942
Stalingrad 1942 (decimated At Stalingrad)
Northern France 1943 (reformed)
Russia 1943
Kiev and Dnepr Bend 1943
Poland 1944
Hungary 1944
Slovakia 1944
Germany 1945

25. Panzer-Division

Formed in February 1942 from units in Norway.
Divisional Insignia:
Activated in 1943 in Russia this division had two signs, but there is no photographic evidence of the more complex second emblem. The most common of this division's sign was a stencil showing a row of three stars over a horizontal line over a modified crescent. This was normally seen applied in either yellow or white, though other colours like and even black were used.
Units:
Panzergrenadier Regiments 146, 147
Panzer Regiment 9
Panzer Artillery Regiment 91
Panzer Aufkl Abt 25
Theatres of Operation:
Russia Southern sector 1943
Kiev 1943
Denmark 1944 (refit)
Poland 1944
Germany 1945

26. Panzer-Division

Formed in 1942.
Divisional Insignia:
This divisional sign was a painted yellow arrow with three bars across the shaft, and was very similar to that of the 22. Panzer-Division. The division saw limited action and was disbanded following heavy casualties in early 1943 at Stalingrad.
Theatres of Operation:
Voronezh and Voroshilovgrad until it was disbanded 15 Feb 1943 and absorbed into 7. Panzer Division and 24. Panzer Division.

APPENDIX IX

Armoured Crew Uniforms

Wearing their special black Panzer uniforms the *Panzertruppen* were very distinctive from the German soldier wearing his field-grey service uniform. The uniform was first issued to crews in 1934, and was the same design and colouring for all ranks of the Panzer arm, except for some of the rank insignia and national emblem worn by officers and Generals. The colour of the uniform was specially dyed in black purely to hide oil and other stains from the environment of working with the armoured vehicles. Across Europe and into Russia these black uniforms would symbolise a band of elite troops that spearheaded their armoured vehicles and gained the greatest fame, or notoriety, from being part of the once-powerful *Panzerwaffe*.

The black Panzer uniform itself was made of high quality black wool, which was smooth and free of imperfections. The uniform comprised of a short black double-breasted jacket worn with loose fitting black trousers. The deeply double-breasted jacket was high-waisted and was specially designed to allow the wearer to move around inside his often cramped vehicle with relative comfort. The trousers were designed to be loose also in order to enable the wearer plenty of movement.

The 1934 pattern Panzer jacket was only in production until it was replaced in 1936 by the second pattern. This pattern was very popular and remained in production throughout the war. It was very similar to that of the first pattern. It had the short double-breasted jacket, normally worn open at the neck, showing the mouse-grey shirt and black tie. But with this design it did not lack the provision for buttoning and hooking the collar closed for protection against weather.

On the jacket the shoulder straps, collar patches and around the death's head skull were piped in rose pink *Waffenfarbe* material. The rose pink piping was worn by all ranks around the outer edge of the jacket collar, but this design was discontinued by 1942. However, members of the 24th Panzer-Division did not wear the rose pink piping, theirs being gold/yellow. This colour piping was purely for commemorative wear and had been originally worn by the 1st Kavallerie-Division, and was the only cavalry division in the German Army to be converted to a fully-fledged Panzer division.

The German national emblem on the double-breasted Panzer jacket was very similar to that worn on the German service uniform. It was stitched on the right breast in heavy white cotton weave, but the quality and colour did vary according to rank. For instance, they were also manufactured in grey cotton yarn or in fine aluminum thread. For officers and Generals of the *Panzertruppen* they were normally heavily embroidered in heavy silver wire.

The jacket was specially designed in order to limit the number of buttons worn on the outside of the coat, except for two small black buttons positioned one above the other on the far right side of the chest. These were stitched into place to secure the left lapel when the jacket was closed up at the neck.

The trousers worn were identical for all ranks. There was no piping used on the outer seams of the trouser legs. Generals of the *Panzertruppen* did not wear the red stripe on the trousers, as they did with the German army service uniform. The trousers did have two side pockets with button down pocket flaps, a fob pocket and a hip pocket. The trousers were generally gathered around the tops of the short leather lace-up ankle boots.

The headgear worn by the Panzer crews in 1941 was the Panzer enlisted man's field cap or *Feldmütze* and was worn by all ranks. It was black and had the early type national emblem stitched in white on the front on the cap above a woven cockade, which was displayed in the national colours. The field cap had a pink soutache.

For the next three years of the war the Panzer arm extensively wore the Panzer field cap. However, in 1943, a new form of head dress was introduced, the *Einheitsfeldmütze*, or better known as the Panzer enlisted man's model 1943 field cap. The M1943 cap was issued in black, but when stocks run low troops were seen wearing field-grey field caps. Both colours of the design were worn universally among Panzer crews and the cap insignia only slightly differed between the various ranks. The field-grey German Army steel helmet was also issued to the *Panzertruppen* as part of their regulation uniform. Generally the steel helmet was not worn inside the cramped confines of a tank, except when crossing over rough terrain and normally when the crewmember was exposed under combat conditions outside his vehicle. Many crews, however, utilised their steel helmets as added armoured protection and attached them to the side of the tank's cupola, and to the rear of the vehicle.

Another item of headgear worn by the Panzer arm was the officer's service cap or *Schirmmütze*. Although this service cap was not technically an item designed for the Panzer arm, it was still nonetheless an integral part of the Panzer officers uniform and was worn throughout the war.

The Panzer uniform remained a well-liked and very popular item of clothing and did not alter extensively during the war. However, in 1942 a special two-piece reed-green denim suit was issued to Panzer crews in areas of operations where the climate was considered warmer than normal theatres of combat. The new denim suit was hard wearing, light and easy to wash, and many crews were seen wearing the uniform during the summer months. The uniform was generally worn by armoured crews, maintenance, and even Panzergrenadiers who were operating with half tracked vehicles, notably the Sd.Kfz.251 series. This popular and practical garment was identical in cut to the special black Panzer uniform. It consisted of the normal insignia, including the national emblem, Panzer death head collar patches and shoulder straps.

Apart from the uniforms worn by the Panzer crews, a special uniform was introduced for both *Sturmartillerie* and *Panzerjäger* units. The uniform was specially designed primarily to be worn inside and away from their armoured vehicles, and for this reason designers had produced a garment that gave better camouflage qualities than the standard black Panzer uniform. The uniform worn by units of the *Panzerjäger* was made entirely from lightweight grey-green wool material. The cut was very similar to that of the black Panzer uniform. However, it did differ in respect of insignia and the collar patches.

The *Panzerjäger* uniform was a very practical garment and it was identical to the cut of the to the *Sturmartillerie* uniform, but with the exception of the colour. The uniform was made entirely of field-grey cloth, but again differed in respect to certain insignia. The collar patches consisted of the death's head emblems, which were stitched on patches of dark blue-green cloth and were edged with bright red *Waffenfarbe* piping. However, officers did not display the death's head collar patches, but wore the field service collar patches instead. No piping on the collar patches was used either.

Like the summer two-piece reed-green Panzer denim suit worn by Panzer crews, both tank destroyer and self-propelled assault gun units also had their own working and summer uniforms, which were also produced in the same colour and material.

Apart from the basic issued items of clothing worn by crews of the Panzer, tank destroyer and self-propelled assault gun units, crews were also issued with various items of clothing to protect them against the harsh climates. By the winter of 1942/43 the German Army had developed a new revolutionary item of clothing for the armoured crews called the parka. The parka was a well-made item of clothing that was well-padded and kept crews warm. Initially the parka was first designed in field-grey with a reversible winter white. But by late 1943 a new modification was made by replacing the field-grey side with a camouflage pattern, either in green splinter or tan water. The coat was double-breasted with the interior set of buttons being fastened to provide additional protection.

APPENDIX X

Camouflage and Zimmerit

In June 1941, when the Germans unleashed their might against the Soviet Union, virtually all equipment was painted in dark grey. During the invasion there were literally thousands of vehicles distributed between the Panzer divisions, and these also included captured British and French vehicles too. These foreign vehicles had been modified for German use and were also repainted in dark grey. Captured Russian vehicles too were pressed into German service, but many of the trucks and cars still retained their original Russian green shade. As for Soviet tanks, these were prominently marked with large crosses and repainted in overall dark grey.

For the first four months of Operation *Barbarossa* the vehicles painted in their overall dark grey camouflage scheme blended well against the local terrain. However, with the drastic onset of winter and the first snow showers at the end of October 1941, Panzer crews would soon be filled with anxiety, as their vehicles were not camouflaged for winter warfare. With the worrying prospects of fighting in Russia in the snow the *Wehrmacht* reluctantly issued washable white winter camouflage paint in November 1941. The paint was specially designed to be thinned with water and applied to all vehicles and equipment where snow was on the ground. The application of this new winter whitewash paint could easily be washed off by the crews in the spring, exposing the dark grey base colour. Unfortunately for the crews the order came too late and the distribution to the front lines was delayed by weeks. Consequently, the crews had to adapt and find various crude substitutes to camouflage their vehicles. This included hastily applying their vehicles with a rough coat of lime white wash, whilst others used lumps of chalk, white cloth strips and sheets, and even hand-packed snow in a drastic attempt to conceal conspicuous dark grey parts. Other vehicles, however, roamed the white arctic wilderness with no camouflage at all.

Following the harsh winter of 1941, the spring of 1942 saw the return of the dark grey base colour on all the vehicles. It was during this period that a number of vehicles saw the return of pre-war dark brown and dark green camouflage schemes. Crews had learnt from the previous year the lessons of camouflage, and survival for these young men were paramount. For this reason many crews began utilising and adding to their camouflage schemes by finding various substitutes and applying them to the surface of the vehicle. This included the widespread use of foliage and bundles of grass and hay. This was a particularly effective method and was often used to break up the distinctive shapes and allow them to blend into the local terrain. Mud too was used as an effective form of camouflage but was never universally appreciated among the crews.

For the first time in southern Russia, in the Crimea and the Caucasus, where the summer weather was similar to that in North Africa, many vehicles were given an application of tropical camouflage, with the widespread use of sand colour schemes, almost identical to those used by the *Afrika-Korps*. In southern Russia in the summer the terrain was very similar to that of a desert and for that reason the vehicles were completed in the tropical colours of yellow brown RAL 8000, grey green RAL 7008 or just brown RAL 8017.

By 1943, olive green was being used on vehicles, weapons, and large pieces of equipment. A red brown colour RAL 8012 also had been introduced at the same time. These two colours, along with a new colour base of dark yellow RAL 7028, were issued to crews in the form a high concentrated paste. The paste arrived in 2kg and 20kg cans, and units were ordered to apply these cans of coloured paste over the entire surface of the vehicle. The paste was specially adapted so that it could be thinned with water or even fuel, and could be applied by spray, brush, or mop.

The dark yellow paste was issued primarily to cover unwanted colours or areas of the camouflage schemes, especially during changes in seasons. These new variations of colours gave the crews the widest possible choices in schemes so as to blend in as much as possible to the local terrain. The pastes were also used to colour all canvas tops and tarpaulins on the vehicles.

The new three-colour paint scheme worked very well on the front lines and allowed each unit maximum advantage, depending on the surrounding conditions. However, within months there were frequent problems with supply. Support vehicles carrying the new paste had to travel so far to various scattered units, even from railheads, that frequently Panzer units never received any new application of camouflage schemes. Another problem was due to the fact that many Panzer units were already heavily embroiled in bitter fighting and had neither the vehicles to spare nor manpower to pull them out for a repaint. Even rear area ordnance workshops were returning vehicles to action at such speed that they only managed time to replace parts, and then send them back to the front with no repaint. A great many number of vehicles never received any paste colours at all, and those that fought on remained in dark yellow, sometimes with crews adapting and enhancing the scheme with the application of foliage and mud.

However, of all the failings, the greatest of them all was actually the paint itself. This proved to be unstable when mixed with water, and even the lightest downpour could cause these new colours to run or wash off the vehicles. Even fuel, which was used to give the paste a durable finish, was at such a premium during the later stages of the war, that units were compelled to use water, waste oil and mixed or other paints. All this caused immense variations in the appearance of the paint schemes and as a consequence there were unusual colours like brick red, chocolate brown and light green. In spite of these variations in colour and the fact that there had become little standardization in the camouflage schemes, occasionally though there were complete units that appeared on the front lines properly painted and marked. However, this was often a rare occurrence, especially by 1944.

Throughout 1944, a further drain on German supplies and resources caused considerable disruption of materials. The paint system on the vehicles was just one of many hundreds of deprivations that were inflicted on the already badly depleted Panzer units. During the last months of 1944, the Panzer supply became critical and lots of vehicles were seen in overall dark yellow.

By this time almost all the new vehicles that had left the last remaining factories for the front lines were in their base colour dark yellow. They never received any further camouflage treatment, other than covering with foliage.

The use of foliage during the last years of the war was extensive. Most vehicles and a large range of weapons attached foliage to break up the distinctive shapes. The Germans were masters in the art of camouflaging their vehicles with branches from trees, grass and hay. In fact, some vehicles carried so much foliage that it was sometimes difficult to determine what type of vehicle they were or what camouflage scheme it had. In the last furious year of the war, foliage had become more important than colours. To the crews, being concealed from aerial attack was the key to survival. As the remnants of the once-vaunted Panzer divisions withdrew across Poland to the borders of the *Reich* the crews did not dare waste any time painting vehicles. The widespread use of foliage helped compensate for this.

Bibliography

Healy, Mark, *Kursk 1943: Tide Turns in the East*. Osprey Publishers, 1992.

Jentz, Thomas L. and Doyle, Hilary L., *Germany's Tiger Tanks. VK45.02 to Tiger II: Design, Production & Modifications*. Schiffer Publishing Ltd., 1997.

Jentz, Thomas L. and Doyle, Hilary L., *Panzer Tracks No.4. Panzerkampfwagen IV – Grosstraktor to Panzerbefehlswagen IV*. Darlington Productions, 1997.

Jentz, Thomas L., *Germany's Tiger Tanks. Tiger I & II:Combat Tactics*. Schiffer Publishing Ltd., 1997.

Jentz, Thomas L., *Panzertruppen. The Complete Guide to the Creation & Combat Employment of Germany's Tank Force, 1933-1942*. Schiffer Publishing Ltd., 1996.

Jentz, Thomas L., *Panzertruppen. The Complete Guide to the Creation & Combat Employment of Germany's Tank Force, 1943-1945*. Schiffer Publishing Ltd., 1996.

Manstein, Erich von, *Verlorene Siege*. Athenäum, 1955.

Mawdsley, Evan, *Thunder in the East: The Nazi-Soviet War, 1941–1945*. Hodder Arnold, 2007.

Nipe, George. *Decision in the Ukraine, Summer 1943, II. SS and III. Panzerkorps*. J.J. Fedorowicz Publishing Inc., 1996.

Spielberger, Walter J., *Panzerkampfwagen Tiger und seine Abarten*. Motorbuch Verlag, 1991 (4th edition).

Spielberger, Walter J., *Sturmgeschütze*. Motorbuch Verlag, 1994 (2nd edition). English edition: *Sturmgeschutz & Its Variants. The Spielberger German Armor & Military Vehicles Series Vol. II*. Schiffer Publishing Ltd., 1993.

Töppel, Roman, "Die Offensive gegen Kursk 1943 – Legenden, Mythen, Propaganda". Dresden: Technical University, 2001 (MA Thesis).

Also available from Helion & Company

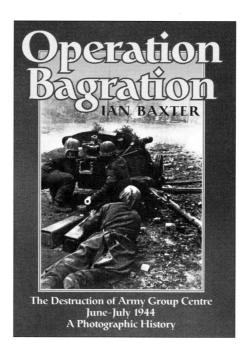

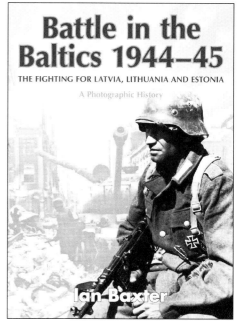

*After Stalingrad
The Red Army's Winter
Offensive 1942-1943*
David M. Glantz
536pp, 117 maps, c 50 photos
Hardback   ISBN 978-1-906033-26-2

*Operation Bagration
The Destruction of Army
Group Centre June-July 1944:
a Photographic History*
Ian Baxter
136pp, c 200 photos
Hardback   ISBN 978-1-906033-09-5

*Battle in the Baltics
The Fighting for Latvia,
Lithuania and Estonia: a
Photographic History*
Ian Baxter
112pp, c 160 photos
Hardback   ISBN 978-1-906033-33-0

A selection of forthcoming titles:

Crucible of Combat: Germany's Defensive Battles in the Ukraine 1943-44
R Hinze   ISBN 978-1906033-39-2

Entrapment: Soviet Operations to capture Budapest, December 1944
K Nevenkin   ISBN 978-1-906033-73-6

*The Last Rally: The German Defence of East Prussia, Pomerania
and Danzig 1944-45, a Photographic History*
I Baxter   ISBN 978-1-906033-74-3

HELION & COMPANY LIMITED
26 Willow Road, Solihull, West Midlands B91 1UE, England
Telephone 0121 705 3393   Fax 0121 711 4075
Website: www.helion.co.uk
Email: info@helion.co.uk